Finishing Life
STRONG

Issues and Inspiration
for Those in the Second-Half of Life!

John Heide

Inspiring Voices®
A Service of Guideposts

Inspiring Voices books may be ordered through booksellers or by contacting:

Inspiring Voices
1663 Liberty Drive
Bloomington, IN 47403
www.inspiringvoices.com
1-(866) 697-5313

ISBN: 978-1-4624-0023-2 (sc)
ISBN: 978-1-4624-0024-9 (e)

Library of Congress Control Number: 2011940548

Printed in the United States of America

Inspiring Voices rev. date: 10/19/2011

Contents

Foreword

So you're past retirement age and you think your usefulness is done.

Wrong!

That's the welcome message of this new study series, *Finishing Life Strong…Issues and Inspiration for Those in the Second-Half of Life* by John Heide.

John Heide's life and ministry make him uniquely qualified to speak on this topic, and he doesn't disappoint. He knows what he is talking about and has a rich tapestry of experience from which to draw. Here, in one place, John draws from that vast experience to compile the best of the lessons he has learned into one helpful, interactive volume.

Addressing "second-halfers," his target group in the second half of their lives, he provides interesting studies on everything from coping with retirement or depression, to interacting beneficially with your grandchildren, or surviving the death of a spouse. His analysis of how second-halfers can cope with the many changes that continually appear—and keep appearing at a much more rapid rate when you are in your second half of life—is humorous, perceptive, and captivating.

If you think life is over for you just because you're older, John's message will grip your heart and give you hope. This is not some positive-thinking book that merely hopes to get older folks feeling better about themselves. Its discussions, points to ponder, teaching and illustrations all tell a compelling story of the ability of people in their second half of life to both enjoy life and to make a difference. The study is chockfull of real-life examples of people who are doing great things for God at an advanced age.

Looking for inspiration and hope? This book is for you. And once you are convinced that God is not through with you, you are not left without direction. You will find numbers of practical and helpful suggestions to get you on the road to a whole new life of excitement in your second half.

You will learn a lot about the interaction of generations and the unique challenges that come with aging. And, most of all, you will probably learn a lot about yourself ... and God's great love and plans for you. Well-researched and making abundant use of Scripture, *Finishing Life Strong...Issues and Inspiration for Those in the Second-Half of Life!* is a groundbreaking study in a user-friendly format.

I encourage you to embark on this exciting journey in the pages that follow.

Ken Horn, Editor, *Pentecostal Evangel*

Introduction

Welcome to the second half of life and ... *Finishing Life Strong*!

Most readers of this book have been born in one century but live in another. With that in mind, consider the following: Ten thousand baby boomers are now signing up for Social Security every day! Each day in America, 11,500 people turn 60 years of age and, with more than 140,000 Americans now over 100 years of age, the United States has its oldest and largest second-half population in history. [1]

Some of you reading this book may live to be 100 years old.

Forty percent of people in the United States are now 50 or older! Read that sentence again! The 40/50 window in America is now wide open ... and millions of people are jumping through it!

Consider also these startling facts: More and more people past 50 are opting to live together instead of getting married. They are reacting to financial considerations such as health insurance, obtaining income and other social benefits, as well as complicated legal entanglements. And, with the absence of a strong moral commitment to marriage, many in the second half of life are now doing what they previously condemned a younger generation for—bypassing marriage.

Believe it or not, the first couple to get married in Manhattan, New York, after gay marriage became legal in July of 2011, were 77-year-old Phyllis Siegel and 85-year-old Connie Kopelov. [2]

Not only are many in the second half less moral than in the past, they are also drinking and using drugs more. Between 2000 and 2008 substance-abuse treatment admissions among those 50 and older increased by 70 percent. In 2008 more than 231,000 individuals over 50 sought treatment. [3] Most people don't like to think about their grandparents having sex outside of marriage or drinking to excess, but it is occurring at alarming rates.

Divorce among the elderly is also on the rise (even among couples 80 years of age and older). This has created a host of new problems for families. When people leave God out of their life at any age they face the consequences of living in a fallen world—without God's help! The results are serious and heartbreaking ... but there is hope!

What This Study Guide Is All About

This manual covers 10 of the most important and requested topics that those traveling through the second half of life find themselves dealing with. These are real life issues. Some are controversial, some encouraging, but all need God's perspective to be successfully navigated. This guide is suitable for personal study or for small-group discipleship and Sunday school classes. Each topic is introduced with a true story or example gleaned from the life of a second-halfer that illustrates the truth of the lesson. The lessons may bring you comfort, and they may challenge you. You may also discover ways to help friends and family members who are facing some of these issues. The book's last chapter provides some brief accounts of people who are accomplishing significant things in their second half of life.

The Bible provides guidance for every life. Each of these lessons includes relevant Bible verses that provide the foundation for understanding and dealing with the topic. They are under the heading Word Faith, because "faith comes by hearing the word of God" (Romans 10:17)!

Questions for discussion and interaction are included, as well as thought provoking Points to Ponder, Points of Action, Information, Group Projects, and Dynamic Revelation highlights which share insights for second-halfers to consider. There are no time limits for finishing each lesson. Take your time as you study, discuss and digest the information.

Satan's last chance to distract, discourage, and detour those who are closer to the finish line will be during the second half of life's race. The purpose of this book and our ministry is to help strengthen every second-halfer in *Finishing Life Strong*! I believe this study will help!

Chapter One

Finding New Direction in the Second Half of Life

Word Faith:

Psalm 32:8; Isaiah 6:8; Isaiah 43:18, 19; Isaiah 30:21

A True Story:

Saracita was 65 years of age. After a busy life, things were finally starting to slow down for her. Saracita and her husband had been farmers for most of their lives and now she was looking forward to spending more time with family and friends. Imagine her surprise when her husband announced to her, "Pack your suitcase, honey. We are moving!"

"Are you kidding," she laughed. "We have so much stuff. There is no way we can move. And besides, think of the deep roots we have here—our church, our many friends and family. Thanks, but I am staying right here!"

Despite her protests, in a few months many of their possessions had been sold or given away. A few things were kept and goodbyes were said. Saracita and her husband embarked on a move to a place hundreds of miles away.

Question:

What would be your feelings if you found yourself moving to a new part of the country at this point in *your* life? Discuss some of the challenges of moving to a new location in the second half of life.

_____

_____

By now, you may have figured out that our story is really referring to a couple in the Bible—Sarah and her 75-year-old husband Abraham. Their story is found in Genesis 12. In the second half of life, Abraham and Sarah found themselves facing new challenges. These included leaving familiar surroundings, going to a strange area, and being surrounded by new people, with no family to welcome them. There was a positive outcome to this story. Because Abraham and Sarah obeyed God and stepped out into this new adventure, a new nation was ultimately formed. Jesus came from that nation!

Not all of us will be asked to uproot our lives and move to another state or country. However, all of us will face new challenges and, perhaps, a new direction in the second half of life. I have friends who, nearing retirement, moved hundreds of miles across the country away from children and grandchildren because God opened a new door of service for them. A move like that requires obedience and sacrifice.

Word Faith Treasure Hunt:

Find the age of the following people when God used them:

Noah (Genesis 7), age: _____
Abraham (Genesis 12), age: _____

Moses (Deuteronomy 34:7; subtract the number of the years he led the children of Israel in the wilderness from his age when he died to get his age when God called him to lead the nation), age: _____ What type of physical shape was he in?

_____

Caleb (Joshua 14:10-12), age: _____

Simeon (Luke 2:25–32), age: _____ (actually his age is unknown, but why may we assume that he was in his second-half of life?)

Anna (Luke 2:36–37), age: _____

Question:

What did Noah, Abraham, Moses, and Caleb in the Old Testament, and Simeon and Anna in the New Testament all have in common?

All of the above had their greatest impact when they were in the "mature" years of life. Just so, God is calling many today to serve Him in their second half!

The Scripture teaches that God does speak to people in the second half of life. I believe that he speaks to adults not in spite of their age, but because of their age! While in many areas age can often disqualify a person from service, God often sees age as preparation for greater service.

"Rosebuds are nice but a beautiful rose in full bloom is a thing of beauty!"

In Acts 2:17, on the day of Pentecost, Peter asserted that in the last days, the young men would see visions and the older people would dream dreams! The dreams that God gave to people in the Bible were not of "yesterday's accomplishments" or "the good old days," but of the future! Daniel and Ezekiel interpreted and received dreams of the future not the past! God wants to give second-halfers vision of what he wants to do today and in the future. One of the ways you can tell if you are trying "full" of the Holy Spirit is that God will continue to give you insights into what He is doing to reach the world and how you can be involved.

Question:

Do you know any second-halfers who are trying something that they had never done before? Do you know anyone to whom God has spoken recently who stepped out in faith into a new ministry?

New Calling:

At age 58, Lewis Jackson became a pastor for the first time. He had been involved in church work for many years but in the second half of life heard God speaking to him about full time ministry. Now he has an effective ministry and is pastoring a growing church in Louisiana. [4]

Be open to God sharing his heart with you about some new changes in store for you in *your* second-half!

A True Story:

Doug Kinne was a successful OB/GYN doctor who at 49 felt God was calling him to a greater work. He left his successful medical practice and entered the second half of life with a desire to train other medical professionals for missions. He developed training materials and became dean of the College of Counseling and Health Care at the Kona, Hawaii, campus of the University of the Nations. At age 58 Doug became ill with cancer and went home to be with Jesus.

Doug finished his race earlier than many other second-halfers but what if he had waited until the normal retirement age to offer himself to God? He would have missed out on having a lasting legacy in the lives he touched. One of Doug's significant quotes from the book written by his wife, Jan, titled *The Finisher*, was this: "The first half of my life I made a living. The second half, I made a difference."

> **"The first half of my life I made a living. The second half, I made a difference."[5]**

Question:

If God called you to be involved in a new ministry in your church, what would you say? _____ How do you think that God would "call" you?

_____

_____

If God spoke to you would you be willing to move somewhere and help plant a church in a new area? _____.

Satan's Deceit:

Believers should ask God what *His* plan is for the second half of their lives. While every person is unique, you should be suspect of any plan or idea that would lead you to disengage from Christian service and cause you to begin focusing on your own individual interests, priorities, and goals. Remember that Lucifer was an angel but chose to focus on his own desires; thus he became Satan, the "Adversary." While God does want us to enjoy his blessings throughout all of life, isn't focusing primarily on ourselves included in the definition of "selfishness"? A preoccupation with one's own happiness is wrong at any age. (See Philippians 2:4.)

Question:

What do you enjoy doing? When you have the time, what are your real interests? What do you get excited about? List and discuss several things:

_____

_____

Any discussion of future service should start with where you are presently. Most people are usually pretty good at what they enjoy doing. They have learned over the years how to be fairly proficient at their hobbies and interests. Whether it is playing an instrument, cooking, quilting, reading, painting, fishing, using the computer, building bird houses, or riding a motorcycle, *you* are pretty good at doing *some* things.

For ministry, three things are needed: 1) Passion; 2) Proficiency; and 3) Opportunity. Identifying what you enjoy doing may be the key to accomplishing something significant for the Lord.

How could your interests and abilities be turned into something that God could use to reach and help others? Ask God to give you insight into how your skills can be used by Him to connect with the next generation or other second-halfers in the community. You can be God's special missionary to touch someone for His glory!

Could you offer to help teach a young person how to play an instrument that has brought you so much joy? Most parents want their children to learn how to play an instrument but cost often prohibits them. Why not offer to share your skills (no matter what level you are) with someone. In turn, this will be a mentoring opportunity for you to share your spiritual values as well as have fun and connect with a younger person.

Could you teach a group of girls how to sew, quilt, or cook?

Do you like to ride motorcycles? Most young men would think you were "pretty cool" if you took them for a ride or shared some stories of the road with them. This would provide a perfect background for sharing your ride through life with Jesus as your guide.

Every person in the second half of life has something to share with the next generation. **DISCOVER** what it is, **DEVELOP** it (you probably already have, or can learn how to be better by taking a class somewhere), and then **DEPLOY** it for your enrichment *and* God's eternal purposes.

Points to Ponder:

How can you (your class or church) start a ministry that uses your interests and skills to help the young people in your church and/or attract other people (young and old) to your church and Christ? Often people are won to Jesus through the door of friendship. Could you bake some cookies for a small group meeting? You'll have lots of friends!

_____

_____

What steps can you take to better equip yourself for finding new direction in the second half of life? _____

_____

A New Direction Physically:

Getting, and staying, in shape (round is not the shape we're looking for...) should be a goal for all of us. Any type of exercise is better than immobility. Get a physical and talk to your doctor about how to keep in shape. If a person feels great, age is not a factor. This would include healthy eating, avoiding destructive habits such as smoking and drinking, and getting proper rest. Park farther away at the store and walk to get some exercise. Don't over do it, but do something to improve your physical condition. The Bible says your body is the temple of the Holy Spirit (I Corinthians 6:19), and taking care of your temple is one way you can bring glory to God.

A New Direction Financially:

Finances can usually be put into two general categories: 1) Saving; and 2) Spending.

Saving:

Most people are never fully prepared financially for the second half of life. It seems everyone could always use more money. Ask yourself: *What resources are available to help me reach my financial goals? Who can help me (people who know how to cut costs and save)?* Do you have a will (even a dated and notarized handwritten copy is better than nothing) that expresses how you want your estate to be dispersed? Perhaps your church could host a seminar such as Dave Ramsey's Financial Peace— which has helped thousands of people to get out of debt. Some adults have resources that can be used to bless the work of God around the world while other second-halfers struggle to make ends meet. One way a church can reach out to other second-halfers would be to have a fund that could help people financially. Starting a "widow's fund" or benevolence ministry could impact lives for Christ! The early church shared their resources with one another and with those less fortunate. (See Acts 2:44-47.)

Spending:

Group project:

What are your spending habits? One interesting test is to track your spending for snack foods, drinks, and so forth, or for small purchases, like a crossword puzzle book or magazine. Keep track of any purchase that is not a "necessity" for one week or thirty days and see how much you spend. Write these purchases down and report back to the group. This could reveal spending habits that keep you "out of money." Discuss how you could cut some of those expenses to free up money for other things.

Watch out for *scams*. There are those who try to make a living out of taking advantage of second-halfers. Before having any major work done on a car, house, or other major repairs or make investments, ask someone you trust about the matter. Churches could have people with skills make themselves available for counsel to second-halfers who have questions in these areas.

Do not get overly involved in trying to win sweepstakes, and other offers of quick wealth. Television and magazine offers abound with new items that can drain second-halfers of needed resources. With many needy social and Christian organizations asking for money, deciding where to give can be a challenge. Having family members or a trusted friend to ask advice from can help you avoid being taken advantage of. Give your resources to organizations that you know are doing what they claim to be doing. Saying *no* to some worthy organizations is difficult but a necessary fact in today's world.

Question:

Have you or someone you know ever been approached by someone attempting to *scam* you or them? How can second-halfers help one another to avoid being taken advantage of? Where is the safest place to invest your resources? (See Matthew 6:19-20.)

Information:

Discuss the following statements. Which one have you used?

"You can't teach an old dog new tricks!" _____

_____.

"You are never too old to learn!" _____

_____.

Which is it? Can we continue to learn or is it too difficult to change? Second-halfers must make sure their attitude doesn't cause them to refuse to learn. Remember, Jesus was only 12 when he challenged the Pharisees in the temple and he began his ministry at 30 years of age. Many of the older Pharisees missed learning from him simply because of his age!

We can learn from those who love and listen to God no matter what their age.

A True Story:

Nola Ochs has the record for being the oldest person to graduate from college. In 2007 she and a granddaughter received their diplomas on the same day as they crossed the stage at Ft. Hays State University Hays, Kansas. Nola was 95 years old and said after her graduation that her goal was to work for a cruise ship and become a storyteller. No doubt, Nola had a lot of stories to share![6]

Another True Story:

At age 73 Bill thought he was just starting to live. So, he made out a game plan for the next 20 years of his life. He wanted to return to college, learn the computer, learn to speak Spanish so he could take some missions trips, and he also put down "learn to play the piano"—something he had always wanted to do!

Both Bill and Nola were into living, not dying. Second-halfers can continue learning and taking advantage of new opportunities in life. How about you?

Finding New Direction Spiritually:

Drawing closer to God in the second half of life will not just happen. Because this is such an important part of *Finishing Life Strong* we have devoted a complete study to this topic in another lesson. As we learned earlier in Acts 2, God wants to give adults a new dream of what He and they can accomplish together. Could it be that, like Esther in the Bible, who God raised up for a specific purpose in His program, God has allowed you to come to this point in your life for just such a time as this? (Read Esther 4:14.)

A New Location:

Where do you want to live the rest of your years? Do you want to remain in the same home or should you move to a new location? Downsizing can help a home to become more manageable and free up time and resources to enjoy other interests. Most second-halfers want to be nearer to family members. What are some of the options? Living in a private home has been the practice for most people. However, in the second half of life, sharing one side of a condo with family members on the other can provide both privacy and security. Adult apartment housing that provides security as well as fellowship and activities can be enjoyed. Retirement communities are popular across the nation. Some second-halfers sell their house, buy a motor home and hit the road full time, working at RV parks in exchange for free lodging. Better yet are those who travel and help build churches across the country. MAPS is the RV ministry of the Assemblies of God that connects second-halfers with church building projects.[7]

Bob Meeks of Bolivar, MO is 81 years young and after retiring from teaching public school he and his wife have been traveling for years helping to build churches and supervise building projects across the country. They want to go as long as they can....don't YOU?

While this sounds exciting, and can be a blessing, it can also pose problems. Looking before you leap is a good practice.

Some second-halfers, due to economic conditions are looking for other seniors who are interested in sharing living arrangements and expenses. Pooling of resources to have a higher standard of living can be a possibility. This option has special challenges that need to be worked through in detail before any decisions are made. In some urban areas the once-used concept of a group home where several people dwell in the same house is being reintroduced. People can bring certain skills to this setting that can add strength and blessing to life. Again, individual expectations and responsibilities should be agreed upon before any permanent decision is made.

Moving closer to a good church can be an option for some, as well as being nearer to services such as stores and medical facilities which can provide second-halfers with security and peace of mind. Many churches have started retirement communities both to serve their congregants as well as reach out to others in the community.

We started this topic with the illustration of Abraham and Sarah who found themselves in the second half of life making a move and finding new direction. Wherever you live, God has a plan for every second-halfer, and it could possibly include some *new direction for you*!

Word Faith:

Psalm 37:25

Question:

Have you found the above verse true in your life? Discuss with others how this verse can apply in the last days of your lives.

_____.

God does not call any of us to sit, but to serve. Where can you serve at *your* age?

With God's presence, age is meaningless. Without God's presence, life is meaningless.

Conclusion:

Why not say this prayer for new direction in your life? "Lord, what do you want me to do with the *rest of my life*? If there is anything new out there for me I want to be open to it. I am available for you to use me however you choose. Here am I Lord ... send me! Amen."

Chapter Two

Retirement in the Second Half of Life

Is retirement a secular or sacred concept? Are there any examples of people retiring in the Bible? What is God's purpose for the retirement years? Will you have enough money to retire? Where should you live? These are important questions that second-half believers want answers to. Creating a Christian Biblical view of retirement requires you to go against the trends of the world and conform your thinking to what the Bible teaches about life in the second half! Read Romans 12:1-2. This lesson will provide some answers—as well as challenges—for those near or in their second half.

Many trace the idea of retirement to the 1930s and President Franklin Roosevelt's introduction of the Social Security program into American life. In 1940, right after Social Security had been adopted, 53.9% of men and 60% of women who reached 21 years of age could expect to live to be 65 and start receiving monthly payments. Today, almost 80% of those who reach 21 can expect to see 65. In 1940 there were approximately 9 million adults who were 65 and older. In 2011-2012, between 36 and 40 million adults are 65 and up, and with more than 140,000 Americans now 100 years of age or older, the second-halfers will continue to rise in numbers and influence for the next 20 years. [8] Four times more people are 65 or older than those who are 18 and younger—a total of some 38 million. There certainly are a lot of "retired" people!

Some believers adamantly say that the word "retirement" is not found in the Bible and that a person should keep going until the Lord calls them home. We would agree that serving the Lord is a lifelong commitment! One old song says, "Sweeter as the years go by." Another states, "The Longer I Serve Him, the Sweeter He Grows!" Can you think of any other songs that talk about serving the Lord for all of life? Why not sing one to begin this study?

Songs: _____.

The numbers are growing. Millions of people find themselves in or soon-to-be in the retirement phase of life! Whether finances permit a person to completely retire or only work part time, everyone in the second-half of life will be faced with similar issues. Let's discover what the Bible says about retirement and then discuss the Seven Steps of Retirement that many second-halfers go through.

It may surprise you (it did me) to discover that the Bible does speak of retirement after years of work.

Word Faith:

Numbers 8:23-26: "And the LORD spake unto Moses, saying, This is it that belongeth unto the Levites: from twenty and five years old and upward they shall go in to wait upon the service of the tabernacle of the congregation: And *from the age of fifty years they shall cease waiting upon the service thereof, and shall serve no more:* But shall minister with their brethren in the tabernacle of the congregation, to keep the charge, and shall do no service. Thus shalt thou do unto the Levites touching their charge." (KJV) (italics mine)

The Message paraphrases the passage: "God spoke to Moses: "These are your instructions regarding the Levites: At the age of twenty-five they will join the workforce in the Tent of Meeting; at *the age of fifty they must retire from the work.* They can assist their brothers in the tasks in the Tent of Meeting, but they are not permitted to do the actual work themselves. These are the ground rules for the work of the Levites." (italics mine)

The Levites were to serve for 25 years and then *retire* from actively doing the physical work they had been doing! Their first career would be over, but their service would continue. (Retiring at 50 years of age … sounds good to me!)

The Levites role would change from the physical work they had been doing to one of helping and mentoring. At age 50 the Levites would use their experience to help prepare the next generation to continue the work of the Lord. The lesson for second-halfers is clear: Yes, there can be retirement from a primary job but new opportunities await everyone to share their lessons from life and make the "rest of our years the best of our years!"

Question:

At what age did you or would you like to retire or stop working from a primary job? _____.

Seven Steps In Retirement:

Many second-halfers will be in one or a combination of these steps. Let's see where you are at in this process.

1. Enchantment:

The anticipation of retiring is, for most, a much-looked-forward-to event. If a person's health is good, who would not look with excitement on not having to get up every morning and trudge off to work? Magazines, television, and other media make retirement appear like a dream come true—with endless cruises, golf, a steady retirement check, help from Social Security, mostly free healthcare through Medicare, and time spent playing with grandchildren or close friends. From the working years to the playing years! Yes, retirement is alluring and enchanting for many!

Question:

How does the media influence our view of retirement?

_____

2. Event:

Next comes the much anticipated day! Like an anticipated wedding, there will come a day when the event takes place. The time clock is punched and the cubicle or tool box is cleaned out. The keys of a transportation vehicle are turned in and the office party is soon over. You are officially "retired." You may even have a gold watch, a plaque, or a nameplate to prove it. You drive home, enter the house and, as the door shuts behind you, you breathe a sense of relief. It's over! You didn't know if you would live long enough to retire. Now for the fun! This step is short but still an achievement to be enjoyed. Like a wedding, the event is soon over and now the retiree is entering a significant time of transition.

Question:

Discuss what happened the day you retired:

---

3. Enjoyment:

The next morning after the event of retirement is such fun! You take a little extra time to drink that cup of coffee (maybe even have two cups), you linger over the morning newspaper and perhaps check the want ads for jobs. You catch yourself chuckling, *Why am I looking at the want ads? I am retired!* The phone rings and it's your best friend.

"Hi, (your name), let's go _____ (you fill in the blank)."

"Sure," you respond, "I have been looking forward to this for a long time." And off you go. *Ah, this is living!*

Sound familiar or at least hoped for? This is an oft repeated story for many new retirees and it is okay ... up to a point. It is only natural to want to take some time doing the things you have only dreamed about doing while you were spending a third or more of your day going to work. Go ahead take a few months to: play, travel, visit the grandchildren, or just do some of the jobs around the house you have been putting off. Unfortunately for many retirees, this becomes the sum of their retirement years.

But for many, especially for the Christian, a nagging questions remains: *Is this all there is to life?*

Question:

Discuss what you did the first few months after you retired. Did you travel? Did you visit family members?

---

4. Disillusioned:

Resorts, cruise lines, and travel agencies have appealing ads that catch the eye of retirees who spend billions of dollars annually enjoying the second half of life! However, after the travel, the fun, and indulgence in lots of good food is over, then what? When the shopping no longer satisfies and the hobby becomes a chore (how many birdhouses or afghans can one make), what's next? Sleeping in, and watching soap operas can get old pretty quick. If physical limitations, financial challenges or relationship issues (divorce or death) become the reality not permitting the fulfillment of the "dream" life, where can the retiree turn for fulfillment? How can one find significance in the second half of life?

Question:

Do you know any second-halfers who tried to find significance by pursuing the "good life" that is portrayed by the media? Did they find it?

---

5. Evaluation:

Right in the middle of the second half of life, what has been described as an identity crisis can happen. It is at this point in life when some eye opening occurs and some hard choices need to be made.

What does a person do when they come to the conclusion that the things they had thought would satisfy simply don't? Most people relate their significance to their work. But when the work is over, where should a second-halfer look for purpose since after a period of time the thrill of doing what we want to wears off? When the revelation comes that the things of this world do not satisfy, there are two reactions people usually have. First, a quest can begin for new things, new hobbies, and greater thrills. The retired person may spend more money and more physical and emotional energy trying to find the "missing fulfillment." Often this search can lead to a downward spiral ending in costly, difficult, and disappointing results. Secondly, a person can ask himself or herself, *Isn't there more to life than just doing things?* That question, or one like it, can lead a person to discover that the only real fulfillment in life comes when they are attaining their purpose for being on earth.

To discover that purpose, a person must go to God and ask Him, "What on earth is going on in my life? What am I here for?" There may be a third response when the thrill of retirement wears off—a person may become depressed at realizing that they may have another 25 years of retirement ahead of them and doing unfulfilling things is not much to look forward to. The fourth topic we will study is on dealing with depression in the second half of life.

Let's take a break:

Halftime in the Locker Room

Many sports have a halftime when the teams take a short break. What goes on in the locker room at halftime can give us insight into how a believer approaches the second half of life. Half time is a time of evaluating how the team did during the first half of the game. The coach discusses what mistakes were made in the first half and what changes should be made when the team goes back to finish the game. The players get some needed rest and are inspired to get back in the game until it's over.

"As long as there is a second half we can win this game!"

Famed UCLA basketball coach John Wooden was reported as saying to his team, "As long as there is a second half we can win this game!" This attitude of winning in the second half needs to catch on among all second-halfers. Wooden's teams won 10 national championships and he had four undefeated seasons. John Wooden died at 99 years of age, a Christian gentleman who made his second half count![9]

Halftime can be a "game changing" event for us if it brings evaluation, rest, inspiration, and getting back in the game of life with renewed excitement. Every person has an opportunity to find greater fulfillment in the second half of life! It is never too late to start doing what is right!

Question:

Was there a time in your life that you had to evaluate where you were at and make some choices that changed your priorities?

6. Discovery:

Realizing that there are more important things in life than just having fun leads every second-halfer to ask these questions: *What do I want to do with the rest of my life? Why am I still alive while others are not? Is there a purpose for me? How can I find it?* The *discovery* time in life can be a fresh understanding of what the remaining years can be or a renewing of a dream that had been long set aside.

A True Story:

Jim was 68 years old. He had always wanted to be a doctor but when he married young he found himself working in an engineering job and remained there for 40 years. He had made a good living for his family, yet, he still found it a thrill and challenge to read about doctors who made a difference in helping people to recover their lives after a debilitating illness.

What did Jim do after he went through some of the steps in this lesson? At 68, he went back to school to study medicine. Jim had to admit that going through 12 years of medical school would put him at 80 years of age and they probably wouldn't let him near a hospital (unless he was a patient). So in 3 short years and at 71 he graduated as a registered nurse. Since graduating, he has made several medical missions trips and is fulfilling his long-delayed dream in the second half of life!

Word Faith:

Genesis 37: 5-10; 43:26; 44:14. In Genesis 37, God gave a dream to a teenager named Joseph of what would happen in his life. However, Joseph did not see the fulfillment of the dream until he was in his 50s. Be encouraged that God may yet fulfill a lifelong desire as you seek his best for the rest of your life!

Something New:

Don't limit yourself to your present abilities. You may have some hidden talents that are just waiting to be discovered and developed. The renowned artist Grandma Moses picked up a paintbrush for the first time when she was 76 years old and did not stop painting until she had finished over 1,000 paintings. She completed 25 paintings after she was 100 years old! Why not pick up a brush, a needle, an instrument, or tool, and see what *you can do*!

Question:

Is there something you have always wanted to try or learn how to do but never "got around to it"? Complete this blank: I would like to try and

_____

What would it take for this to become a reality in your life?

_____

Personal Impact:

If you have not accepted Jesus into your life, asking him to help you would be a great way to start *your* second half! Here are the ABCs of accepting the Lord in your second half.

A— Admit that you have lived much of your life trusting in your own abilities and not asking God's help (the Bible calls that sin, something we have all done).

B— Believe that Jesus has a plan for the rest of your life and that you need his forgiveness for living life on your own terms. Christ's death on the cross enables God to forgive you and bring you into his family. (See John 1:12.)

C— Commit the rest of your days to God for his direction and help! Prayer is the best way to start the day off—giving each day to God. See what He will do and what opportunities you will have to help others!

Your primary purpose in life is to have a relationship with the one who gave you life...God. Oswald Chambers stated: We are not destined to happiness, nor to health but to holiness...at all costs a person must have the right relationship with God.[10] Do you have that right relationship with God? Your secondary purpose in life will be found when you have the Lord directing you to where you can make the greatest contribution for the rest of your life! That brings lasting joy and significance!

7. **Excitement**:

Discovering and developing new skills can bring new opportunities and a sense of accomplishment and expectation for future challenges. The "I can do this" attitude is a great source of energy and excitement for second-halfers!

Questions:

How could the church help second-halfers to discover or develop their skills?

_____

Could the church provide opportunities that use the skills of second-halfers in the community? Perhaps inviting a retired doctor, nurse or appliance repairman to come and share with second-halfers tips could provide both a service and a way to connect with the professional.

_____

Could the church offer pre-retirement counseling to help prepare people for this important transition?

_____

Conclusion:

God's plan for retirement is for each person to have a fulfilling second half of life. Read Job 42:12. A life where you are able to look back through your years, gather all of your work, social, and spiritual experiences, and transform them into a life message. That message can be shared with those around you and passed on to those coming after you!

Retirement can be turned into "returnment" as you give back to others what you have learned over a lifetime.

Finding what you want to do during the second half of life deserves careful pre-planning and thoughtful prayer. Just as second-halfers are encouraged to pre-plan their finances, health care options, and even burial arrangements, those getting close or entering into their retirement years should seriously think about what they want to do, how they will be able to do it, and where they want to live to accomplish God's plan.

Talking to a trusted friend, a pastor, or others who are "retired" can provide some needed and helpful information.

Hundreds of Christian organizations are looking for second-halfers to join them and make a difference around the world. Short-term missions trips, both in the U.S. and abroad, are available for second-halfers to use whatever talents they have.

Retirement brings changes and challenges to everyone. How you fill the hours and days that had been spent in working to make a living, how you "live to leave a legacy," is how you will be remembered, how you *Finish Life Strong*!

Chapter Three

Raising and Reaching Your Grandchildren for Christ

Ask any parent about their children and they will mention how many they have. But ask any grandparent about their grandchildren and they will quickly tell you how many they have, their ages, their names, and perhaps pull out their billfold, or phone (if they are into technology), and show you pictures of them. This chapter discusses one of the major issues that impacts millions of second-halfers across America today—raising grandchildren. Also of major concern for Christians is how to influence and reach grandchildren for Christ. How can you leave them a legacy of our faith and values?

A True Story:

Marlene lives in the West Monroe, Louisiana, area and has raised both her granddaughter *and* great granddaughter! When her unmarried granddaughter followed in her mother's footsteps, became pregnant and was unable to raise the child, Marlene and her husband volunteered to adopt the child. Marlene is now raising her great-granddaughter Ashton who, at 13 years old, is doing well in a Christian school. Marlene's husband died four years ago leaving Marlene the primary parent for Ashton. Marlene also is the bookkeeper for the church she attends. Oh, by the way, Marlene is *82 years young!* When told she does not look her age, Marlene comments, "Adopt a teenager and they will keep you young!" This lady deserves several gold medals for she has been doing something that exceeds what any star athlete is likely to ever accomplish. Marlene is a true example of someone who is leaving a legacy in the life of her family.

Word Faith:

Second Timothy 1:5 records the story of Eunice and Lois, a mother and grandmother who influenced Timothy for Christ. Their faith must have left a lasting legacy and imprint on his life, as well as on others who noticed him. If we take the TIME (one way of spelling LOVE) and try to become creative in our ways of being involved in their lives, we can leave a lasting legacy on our grandchildren. Remember, it all starts with prayer, but it doesn't end there!

In years past, a visit to grandparents was often limited to Thanksgiving, Christmas, and perhaps a short time in summer. Grandparents may not have been as involved in their grandchildren's lives as they are today.

Question:

Did you ever spend time at your grandparents when you were young? What were some of the experiences you remember about those visits? Do your grandchildren come to visit you?

_____

_____

I know a lady whose five grandchildren (ages 6, 7, 8, 9, and 10) spend every Saturday morning with her. (She usually needs to rest after they leave, but it does give her a few hours each week with them).

Today's grandparents may find themselves going to soccer games (and pretending to know what's going on), dance recitals, music lessons, and a host of other activities their grandchildren are involved in. Another indicator of today's society is that over 6 million children under 18 are being raised by their grandparents. Many more grandparents are actively involved in their grandchildren's day-to-day lives.[11] These "grandfamilies" are increasing as grandparents step up to help or raise their grandchildren.

6 million children under 18 are being raised by their grandparents.

Question:

Do you know anyone who is raising their grandchild? What special challenges do they face?

Raising grandchildren is a difficult task in today's world. There are many negative influences from the media, school, other family members, and peer pressure. Just trying to keep up with and relate to today's young people can be exhausting. For grandparents to counteract negative forces takes God's wisdom and much prayer.

The church can come to the aid of grandparents who are raising their grandchildren by offering classes on child raising, perhaps providing some occasional relief by taking the grandparent out for a meal, or offering to take the child for a day or on a short trip. The church can come along side grandparents and make sure that grandchildren are involved in all of the programs for young people that are possible. Having a younger, positive male or female role model can help strengthen the grandparents goal of providing a spiritual environment for their grandchildren.

Question:

Does your church encourage participation by all children in their programs? Some may need some financial help to be included. Could the youth programs become a good outreach in the community by promoting the program as a source for help for those grandparents who are raising grandchildren?

Whether it is driving grandchildren to school or going with them on a class trip, today's grandparents have a wonderful opportunity of passing on their faith to the next generation. This can start with helping to lead your grandchild into a relationship with Jesus! Let's discuss some ways that may help bring your beautiful grandchild to Christ.

1. Stay Connected:

Whether you live near to your grandchildren or miles apart, modern technology makes it possible to connect with them much easier than years ago when visits might be limited to only once or twice a year.

If you do not live near your grandchildren you can stay connected through the mail. Send birthday cards and cards on other special days to them. If they achieve an honor or award, use that occasion to let them know they are special. Always include the truth that God has given them their abilities and you are proud of them for developing their skills. If you use the computer, use email or other Internet social programs to connect with them. If you know how, you can text them on their cell phone. They will respond to a text or email much quicker than a letter or "snail mail." Use of new technology (Skype, Web cams, etc.) where you can see and interact with your grandchildren on the computer helps to shorten the distance and keep you visually connected. Of course, you can try calling them on the telephone; some may take time to talk! As a personal reminder you may want to put down on the calendar a day every month or quarter that you will try to make a contact with your grandchildren.

If you have several grandchildren this could be a full-time job so you may want to space them out by contacting them every other month. This is work, but God has you in their lives for a reason—and aren't they worth it?

2. Surprise Visits:

If possible, arrange to have lunch with your grandchildren at their school. Most schools will allow grandparents to come by for a visit. If you have had an interesting experience (travel or work), you can probably speak to their teacher about coming and sharing with the class. Guess who will be especially proud to have grandma or grandpa come to their school? Surprise them with a small gift or call.

3. Do Something Together:

Why not do some work together with your grandchildren? Ask for their help. Whether it is raking leaves, baking cookies, washing dishes, or painting a house, working together helps to unite people. And it is a good opportunity for you to share some of your stories and discern what is going on in their life. Sometimes grandchildren will listen more to grandparents than their parents so use this opportunity to share your faith with them. Telling how God is helping you at this point in your life will instill in them the concept that God will also be around for them when they get older. Once, as my grandson and I were doing something together, he said to me, "Grandpa, I like you the best!" I am not sure who or what he was comparing me to but I sure enjoyed hearing it!

4. Prayer Makes the Difference:

Pray regularly for your grandchildren that God will touch their lives. Bring their names before God often. Whether you ever see the answers to your prayers in your lifetime is not why you pray for your grandchildren. Prayer sows seeds that will bear eternal fruit. God hears *your* prayers!

A True Story:

"Grandpa didn't quit praying!" A veteran missionary recounted that in his early years he rejected God, left home, and had no contact with his grandparents for 17 years. When he came back to the Lord at age 28, he went and visited his godly grandparents. They were thrilled and his grandmother told the young man, "Your grandfather has prayed for you every day for the past 17 years." Wow! The missionary stated that he believed that he came back to Christ because Grandpa didn't quit praying. What an encouragement for us to "not quit praying" for as long as it takes to see our grandchildren come to Christ.

Memory books are great tools that help you to recall your earlier years. Experiences can be written down and presented to your grandchildren. [12] You can also write down your personal testimony of how you came to Christ and share your spiritual values you want to pass on to them. Do you remember reading a card or letter over and over again that you received from someone you loved? So will they!

Question:

Does your church have a Grandparents Day? The first Sunday after Labor Day in September has been designated as Grandparents Day.

This is a great opportunity to bring your grandchildren (and perhaps their parents) to church, and possibly include lunch afterwards. This once-a-year celebration can build great memories and be used by God to touch their lives. This can also be a great outreach event for a local church. Some churches have a photo opportunity for families, prepare a special meal, or honor a Grandparent of the Year during this time. For more information on having a Grandparents day go to: **www.50alive. com.**[13]

What are your grandchildren's interests? Let them become your interests! You may not like their music or games but you can look for talent and try to understand what they are talking about.

TWP to Pray

Someone once said that before we have earned the right to *pray* with young people, we may have to first **Talk** with them, **Walk** with them, **Play** with them. Then, finally, we get to **Pray** with them!

Talk: Jesus loved children and laughed with them. How else would they have come to Him and spent time with Him? Learn to laugh with your grandchildren. Every generation has their own language and although it can be difficult understanding some of today's terminology, grandparents must keep the lines of communication open to reach the minds and hearts of their grandchildren. Younger children's hearts are usually tender toward spiritual truth. They can believe and accept Jesus.

Walk: Spend time with them, going to the zoo or a ballgame, fishing, shopping, or doing other things that cause you to laugh together. Tell your grandchildren what things were like when you were young, including some of the struggles and how the Lord helped you through that time in your life. Sharing failures as well as successes make a grandparent sound real and gives hope to a struggling young person.

Play: Doing fun things together creates a neutral area where you can often pass on lessons from life without sounding like you are lecturing or preaching. Most of all, enjoy each other.

Not Recommended: We would not recommend trying to skateboard or rock climb with your grandchild. Perhaps the Baby Boomer grandparents may be brave enough, but not me—and I am a Baby Boomer!

Pray: When you have taken the first three steps, you can believe God to bring this final opportunity! This is every grandparent's goal and a delight when your grandchild will pray with you. When they allow you to pray with them, you know you have formed a good relationship and are leaving a legacy in their lives that the Holy Spirit will use. You have planted good seeds and now continue to water them by praying with and for them.

Question:

How can you implement the Talk, Walk, Play to Pray concept with your grandchildren?

_____

Perhaps two grandparents could "team up" to help their grandchildren.

All of the ideas we have been discussing have two goals: to enjoy the grandparenting experience and to connect with your grandchildren so that ultimately they may come to know the greatest treasure: Jesus!

Have a "Passing the Baton" ceremony. Get a short wooden dowel or baton (like they would use in a relay race) and at a family gathering (or it could be sent through the mail) briefly tell everyone you have a gift for your grandchild. Make this event a *big deal*! Tell your grandchild that the baton represents all of your values, what you would want to give them if you could. It might include "faith, hard work, honesty, integrity, purity, love, respect"—whatever you believe is important. After your "speech," present the baton to your grandchild. If you want to make a real impression on them have their name engraved on the baton or some special decoration they would like. This could be done with a ring, a necklace, or whatever is meaningful to your grandchild. The idea is to have a presentation ceremony that makes them feel special and causes them to realize that you are giving them something very valuable—your life's lessons and values! This event does not have to be long to be significant. Conclude with a brief prayer. They will remember and treasure your gift and God will use this experience to serve as a "memorial" of your faith and values you are passing along to them.

Plant a tree or some flowers or a shrub in your grandchild's name. They will remember and be honored to have their own plant.

Get Some Help:

If you know a person in your church or a friend who you feel could relate to your grandchild, don't hesitate to ask them to come over to meet them. If your grandchild is into motorcycles and you know a person who rides (and would be a good influence), try to make the connection. Touching your grandchild's life for Christ is what needs to happen. It doesn't matter who helps you get it done.

Grandparents can leave something *for* their grandchildren or something *in* them! Leaving an earthly inheritance *for* grandchildren is a great thing. Leaving a legacy of our faith and love *in* them is the best and most lasting thing you can do.

Conclusion:

Spend time praying for your grandchildren by name. Pray that God will lead them to people who can have a positive influence in their lives and some who will point them to Jesus! Could you be the answer to someone who is praying for their grandchild? Names:

Additional Helps:

Here are some resources with a variety of information from legal issues to physical, social and spiritual, concerns for grandparents:

> http://www.grandmabetty.com (One of the best all around sights with tons of information)
> http://www.raisingyourgrandchildren.com/Index.htm
> http://www.usa.gov/Topics/Grandparents.shtml
> http://www.crosswalk.com/family/parenting/leading-your-grandchild-to-christ-11579516.html

Chapter Four

Dealing With Depression in the Second Half of Life

A True Story:

Driving home toward Ozark, Missouri, from Joplin on Monday night May 23, 2011, Jim and Ramona Brame believed the worst was over. The couple had spent all day helping their son, Dale, his wife, Angel, and their 12-year-old son, Jamie, pick up the pieces of what was left of their Joplin home. An F5 tornado had roared through the city Sunday evening destroying almost 7,000 homes and becoming the deadliest tornado in American history.

On Monday, Jim and Ramona, along with other friends and family, spent most of the day salvaging anything they could find. "We got five good loads out of there (Monday). We were tired and just wanted to come home and crash," Jim Brame said. "But that didn't happen."

As Jim and Ramona drove toward Ozark, lightning bolts shot across the sky. One of those bolts may have set their house afire about 8 p.m. Monday. By the time Ozark firefighters responded, the Brames' two-story home was ashes.

When they reached their driveway, they knew something was wrong. The lights of fire engines lit the long driveway. Firefighters were putting out the flames of what used to be their home.

Dale said he was having a hard time believing what had happened to his family within 24 hours. Ramona was also struggling to find an answer. "The good Lord has something against the Brames' homes," she said. "He destroyed them both."

She recalled some of the things she lost in her home: her grandma's china, an old sewing machine, family heirlooms. "We lost all the Brame pictures. Ours got burnt, and theirs blew away," she said.[14]

After their losses, who could find fault with the Brame family for being depressed?

Where do you find the strength to rise out of a terrible situation to face life with a smile and resolution to keep going forward? Can you avoid becoming depressed when life comes crashing in on you? Where is God when things go wrong? What does the Bible say about depression and how you can face the future? This chapter addresses an issue that every person will face. Whether it is the result of a literal storm, or a financial, physical or family storm, everyone at one time or another can be depressed. Thankfully no one is left on their own to figure out an answer. The one who created us also gives insight on how to deal with and overcome depression.

Question:

What were some of the feelings you think the Brame family experienced?

Information:

Next to heart disease depression may be the second leading cause of death in today's world. Depression is no respecter of age, education, or social standing, and can impact anyone's life at seemingly unsuspecting times.

The National Institute on Mental Health gives the following information regarding depression:

There are almost 20 million Americans who suffer from some form of depression.

Thirty-percent of women are depressed and men's rates, traditionally much lower, are climbing at a rapid rate.

Pre-school children are the fastest growing market for anti-depressants.

More information on depression can be found at: http://www.nimh.nih.gov/index.shtml[15]

Question:

Why do you think more women are depressed than men? (The answer should not be, "because they are married to them!") Why do you think preschoolers would be depressed and need antidepressants?

Depression is thought to cost employers over 50 billion dollars a year in lost productivity due to high absenteeism in the work place. Depression is now being linked to major heart disease as well as many other physical problems.

Most people understand times of crisis or tragedy cause a person to be subject to depression more than in normal times in life. The Holmes and Rahe Stress Scale study lists the death of a spouse as the leading cause of depression. It earns 100 points in their study which links physical illness to major events in a person's life.

Many in the second half of life have lost someone close to them. In marriage, typically, the longest to survive is the wife. Of the more than 140,000 Americans who have reached 100 years of age, nine out of 10 are women. While the gap is narrowing, life expectancy rates still give the edge to the ladies at almost 80 for the women and a little over 76 for the men.

Humor: When asked why men die sooner than women one older gentleman responded: "Maybe they want to!"

While there are many factors including life style and behavior, diet and exercise patterns, stress, and more that can impact statistics, generally you will find more second-halfers among the ladies than men in a local church. See chapter 5, "Surviving the Death of a Spouse," for more information.

Question:

In your church or group, are there more women in their second half than men? How does this impact the church?

_____

_____

What could the church do to better meet the needs of those who have lost a spouse?

_____

Do you have any ideas on how the church could reach out to welcome more men and women who have lost a spouse?

_____

THE BIBLE AND DEPRESSION

Word Life:

Psalm 42:5 and 11 and 43:5 all contain the words "Why are thou cast down O' my soul and why are you disquieted within me?" (KJV). Three times in 12 verses those words are repeated. *The Message* paraphrase uses "down in the dumps" and "crying the blues" to describe depressing times.

Question:

What does being down in the dumps mean to you? What are some other terms used for being depressed?

Whatever we call it, most of us in the second half of life have experienced being depressed at some time in our life. As we grow older and experience some of the normal changes in life, the "seasoned citizen" should be aware of some of the causes and cures for depression.

People in the Bible experienced depressing times and personal tragedies. Let's see how they dealt with depression.

Word Faith:

In I Kings 19, Elijah, fresh from a great victory on Mt. Carmel against the prophets of Baal, soon found himself running from the threats of Queen Jezebel. During his escape he quickly became physically, mentally, and spiritually exhausted. His efforts seemed futile and he came to a point of hopelessness resulting in his request to die (verse 4). He was depressed!

Point to Ponder:

Physical and mental exhaustion can lead to depression.

Lack of proper rest or diet, or emotional overload can result in "throwing a physical or mental breaker" (like a fuse) that results in lack of sufficient power for living. The result can be depression. If you look at what you can no longer do because of physical limitations you can become depressed.

In the opening illustration, the family from Ozark, Missouri, experienced several things that Elijah went through. Both families appear to be physically and mentally exhausted from their recent experience. Think of those who have been in a major storm such as a tornado, flood, or earthquake. Besides the physical loss of property, there can also come a loss of ability to handle the problems mentally and with continued pressure on a person's body and mind; the result can be depression! Family relationships, physical challenges, job losses and many other aspects of life can be a source for depression. At times it seems, *life can be depressing!*

Question:

Have you ever been so tired physically or emotionally that you can relate to Elijah's request to die?

_____

What is the answer? How did Elijah rise out of his depression? What did God use to help lift Elijah's spirits and help him to refocus on the future? God let Elijah sleep and then he sent a raven to bring him a meal. On the surface, sleeping and eating appear too natural to provide a solution for depression. However, both a meal and some rest ended up being just what Elijah needed to get victory over his depression. It is hard to see things clearly when you are physically and mentally exhausted. Major decisions made in this state of mind can be disastrous.

Question:

At what time of day are you usually more mentally alert?

_____ .

Dinner and a movie:

Sometimes people look for God to step in with a cloud of glory and lift us up above the situation. In reality, God may use things very near to you to give you just what is needed. A grandchild's smile, a pet's unconditional love, a fishing trip, a beautiful flower or even a nice meal and enjoyable movie—all simple things but they may help to get beyond the immediate crisis and see the situation in a different way.

Question:

Can you think of some small thing that has helped you during a depressing time in your life?

Suicide and the Second Half of Life:

Suicides are higher among those in the second half of life than any other group.[16] Changes in health, finances, relationships and other aspects of life can weigh heavily on a person. There are many reasons why someone decides to take their life. Usually, a person does not really want to die. However, the pressure of the moment and the inability to see any change or hope in the circumstance, makes death seem to be the only way out.

Most of us know of good people who in a rash moment decided to take their life and their action left many people hurt, with many unanswered questions. How accountable was the person at the moment they took their life? Can a believer still go to heaven and commit suicide or do they immediately go to hell? What is God's view of suicide?

The Scriptures do not deal specifically with the issue of suicide. Psalm 139:13-16 and Jeremiah 1:5 reveal that God is the giver of life and knows every person before they are born. Jeremiah 29:11 shares that God wants good for people. John 10:10 teaches that God wants us to have an abundant life but that the enemy of God's people wants to steal, kill and destroy as many as possible. The Devil magnifies problems to seem overwhelming—and people look for a quick solution. As with Peter, who sank in the water, the waves of life can at times be overwhelming. (Matthew 14:30) However, suicide is a permanent answer to a temporary problem.

As a believer we should seek to trust God and let him give us the Philippians 4:7 experience. Please read that verse! Learning to let the Word of God shape your emotions is difficult but the Holy Spirit will help apply the Scriptures to your life.

Suicide is not the answer. God is the ultimate judge and knows each person's mental and spiritual condition and we leave eternity to

His wisdom. First Corinthians 10:13 encourages you that "there is no temptation that a person is going through that others have not also gone through." We are not alone in the struggles of life. Situations may change but God promises that "God will make a way of escape from the temptation," and that includes the temptation of suicide. It may surprise some readers but many people are tempted at one time or another to commit suicide! It may be just a fleeting thought but the devil will try anything to defeat God's people. When going through a tough time try to have a one or two year outlook. For most people things will be very different in just a few months. Hopelessness can change to joy, defeat can turn to victory. You may get a new job, start a new relationship and be better off than you are at the moment.

Every believer must win the battle of the mind

God will help us in our time of desperation. He can change the *situation* or He can change *us*. When a believer goes through a tough time he is given a testimony that will bring glory to God. Every believer must win the battle of the mind and that is where the Word of God becomes vital to our mental health. Read Isaiah 26:3; Philippians 2:5; I John 4:4; Hebrews 13:5.

When You Suffer From Depression:

Make sure you are getting sufficient rest, eat some good (and healthy) food, and let your body be renewed.

Word Faith:

Read Romans 12:1-2 about renewing your mind. Psalm 19:7 shares how the Word of God can restore and renew your soul (mind). Matthew 11:28 states that Jesus welcomes all who are weary, tired, stressed out and even depressed, to come to him for rest. The rest the Lord can give is a renewing rest that no amount of sleep can provide.

Pause for Prayer:

Lord, I need some rest—rest in the natural and rest in the spiritual. I turn everything that is going on in my mind and life over to you right now. I rest completely in you. Thank you for the grace, peace, and strength that you will give to me. Amen!

Example:

In many Teen Challenge (the Christian drug recovery program) centers, the residents who are trying to recover from a life of drugs and alcohol abuse, are read the Word of God over and over to help them get God's perspective. The "cold turkey" approach to deliverance is strengthened as their minds are restored through the Word of God. People who are drugged with depression can find new insight and strength from God's Word.[17]

Get Involved in Something Bigger Than You:

One of the best ways to overcome depression is to get involved in someone else's life or a project that needs you! Depressed people tend to focus on their circumstances and their immediate problem at hand. Becoming involved in someone else's need seems to lift one's own burdens. The problem may still be there but the outlook has been changed and the individual can gain new insight into his or her own life by sharing with others.

Question:

How can you get involved in helping or reaching out to someone else who also has a need? What are some needs or special projects in your area that could use some of your input? How can you offer help to someone who is going through a period of depression? Their name: _____ Their need: _____.

Second-halfers experience a number of losses in life that could lead to depression. Looking at what you once did but are no longer able to do can be frustrating. Focusing on your abilities and not your limitations is something that each person must work at continually. Learning new ways of adjusting to life's inevitable changes can bring greater significance. Second-halfers are showing great ability to adapt to the ever-changing world of technology by learning new computer and cell phone skills.

Question:

What are some things you can no longer do in your second half of life?

_____

_____

Question:

What are some things you can still do now that you are in the second half of life?

_____

_____

Word Faith:

Psalm 46:1 King David was prone to periods of depression. He was hounded, hunted, and harassed by enemy nations and sometimes those closest to him. He was sought after until he had to hide in a cave from his own people who wanted to kill him. However, David knew that in his trouble God was ever present.

Psalm 57:1 David knew where he could find strength during depressing times.

Where can we go when "calamities" or tragedy come into our lives? For the believer we can put our trust in the Lord. He does offer us a place to hide. Note that David had in mind that his problems were temporary; there would come a time when they would pass.

Psalm 91:1 We will not be spared tough times but we can, with God's help and presence, overcome depression.

Word of Caution:

There can be physical causes that impact our moods. As the body changes with age a chemical imbalance in the brain can cause some types of depressed feelings. A prolonged period of depression may need the input of a qualified doctor to see if there are physical causes to the depression.

A good medical checkup for those in the second half of life can bring answers and relief. However, though medication may be the most used solution, it is not always the best solution. In reality some medications may help bring on depression. God is our best source for lasting peace of mind and joy in life.

Question:

Do you know any people who are over medicated? What are some of the results of using too much medication?

Point of Action: Invite a local pharmacist to come and share the benefits and dangers of medications. Ask the person coming if your second-halfers could bring their medications for an evaluation. Invite outsiders to come to this meeting...not too many!

Conclusion:

The story of Job, with all of his losses, rivals any modern story of personal tragedy. After losing everything, like Elijah, Job wished for death. However, after spending time in God's presence and getting the bigger picture in view, Job found new direction for his life. Life became worth living. In Job 42:12 we read that "God blessed the second half of Job's life more than the first!" For those in the second half of life, God has a plan and purpose. Depression may indeed come. But, with God's help, it can also go—as we seek to find a place of service to others the rest of our life.

The Brame family, who lost their home in a fire, did not lose *everything*: The wife said that the most important thing was that the family was safe, despite their tragedies. "We're really fortunate," Ramona said. "There's a lot of people who aren't."

Prayer:

Lord, each of us is human and life can bring things our way that can cause distress, fear and depression. But, You have promised that You are by my side; and even when I am alone I don't have to be lonely because Your Word says You are with me always and Your grace is sufficient for me. Jesus, all of life is a learning process and I am still learning to lean on You. Through the years and the tears with You by my side I can still have a deep abiding joy and peace that passes understanding. When I look to You I realize, greater is He that is in me than he that is in the world, and with Your help I will *Finish Life Strong*! Amen!

Chapter Five

Surviving the Death of a Spouse

The Holmes and Rahe Stress Scale lists the death of a spouse as the greatest cause for stress in a person's life. [18] While both men and women go through the experience of losing a spouse, far more women find themselves living alone than men. Consider these statistics: Of all the older persons living alone, more than 6.5 million—77%—are women. By the year 2020, this total will be 13.3 million and 85% of those will be women. Between the ages of 65 and 74, 77% of women living alone are widows, while those 75 or older are 88% female. With the 140,000 adults who are now 100 years or older, the statistics rise to nine out of ten who are women.

While the death of a spouse can impact the health, social relationships, housing and employment of a second-halfer, another area that is deeply affected is finances. Almost half of women who survive the death of a spouse are considered poor or near the poverty level. Individual believers, small groups and churches have a tremendous opportunity to reach out to this growing number of men and women.

Question:

If you are doing this study with a group, how many in the group have gone through the experience of losing a spouse? How many are men compared to women? In your church or friends what is the ratio of men to women who have lost a spouse?

Illustration:

Bob and Sally had worked hard all of their lives. Raising three children on a plumber's salary was hard at times, yet they had scrimped and saved and somehow managed to help put all three children through college. Now they were actively involved in their grandchildren's lives. They had also looked toward the future faithfully, setting aside a small yet consistent amount toward their retirement. When they were 30, retirement seemed a distant dream, but now, in their 60s, both Bob and Sally were making serious plans to enjoy their later years. Bob also tried to keep in physical shape. He had enjoyed running when in college, but had given it up because of his busy life. He had recently taken up the practice once again in his late 50s. One morning while out for his usual three-mile run, he felt an uneasiness in his chest. He was used to some discomfort and was not one to give in to pain, so he finished his run. When he got home he sat down in the kitchen and began reading the morning newspaper. At 8:10 am, Bob died of a massive heart attack. He was not overweight, he did not drink or smoke, and he ate healthy. Yet at 64 years of age Sally's life was completely changed. Their plans of retirement were over. No travel, no visiting grandchildren, no quiet walks, everything was just *no*! After 45 years of marriage, what would Sally do now?

The death of a spouse in the second half of life brings a new set of challenges that most have not thought of, much less prepared for. Some couples are forced to plan ahead for this event because of a longstanding illness or health condition. They dutifully get all their business affairs in order, make out their will, perhaps even plan their funeral service. Yet, when death takes place, the whirlwind of choices, changes, and new circumstances are numbing and initially overwhelming.

Is There a Difference When People Die?

Let's go back to Bob and Sally's story. I did not mention that Bob served as a deacon in their local church and had worked with the church youth group for 25 years. He was a faithful follower of Jesus as well as a dedicated husband and father.

Question:

Should Bob's death be viewed differently than had he not known Christ?

Word Faith—What the Bible Says About the Death of a Believer:

Psalm 116:15, I Thessalonians 4:13-18, Philippians 1:21, II Corinthians 5:6-9, John 11:25-26.

Point of Action:

Write down some one-word or short statements about the death of a person.

When a person who knows Christ dies they ...

When an unbeliever dies they ...

Questions:

Do you know someone like Bob and Sally whose plans for enjoying retirement were cut short by death?

For those who know someone or who have lost a loved one:

What were your initial feelings when someone you loved died?

How did your family or friends support you in the first week after a loved one died? What about six months later?

How did or do you cope during the special days when you may be alone (birthdays, anniversaries, holidays)?

_____

What would you say to those who are going through the death of a spouse right now?

_____

How long should a person grieve over the loss of a spouse? What are healthy actions and what would be an unhealthy response to the death of a spouse?

_____

For those in the second half of life, the death of a spouse will have a profound impact. Loneliness, heartbreak, guilt and anger, among other feelings, can keep the surviving person's emotions in turmoil. Many couples who have been married a long time can hardly remember what it was like *not* to be married. They have traveled down a long road of experiences together. Perhaps they went to school together, raised children, had grandchildren, shared houses, and major moves. They certainly shared some losses and gains along the journey. When death occurs a flood of past experiences will fill the survivor's mind and the realization that there will be no more such memories made can be overwhelming. Even if the marriage was not as lengthy as others, the strong ties of love and affection will certainly affect the survivors mind and they will need support and encouragement. It is certainly all right to reminisce about the many shared experiences you had together. Some spouses may even find themselves speaking to their departed spouse in a conversational manner. Realizing our loved one is with Jesus can bring great comfort. Their race is finished and they have won! If the spouse was not a believer there will be more sadness but focusing on the surviving family and friends to become ready to meet the Lord should become our ministry.

Adult children should understand that it takes time to work through the emotional issues when the death of a spouse occurs. If there has been a long illness before death, the caregiving spouse may feel some guilt at the sense of relief that comes with the passing of the spouse. Thoughts such as, *If only I had done something different*, may add to the emotional conflict. These thoughts need some time to be processed and worked through. Encouraging the survivor to "get on with their life" will come in time but should not be rushed.

Becoming a good listener to those who want to talk about their loss is a great opportunity for second-halfers to be God's ministers to the grieving. Sometimes the gift of our presence and just being there may be the greatest thing a grieving person needs. When our words of comfort fail, praying with the person can bring God and his peace to a grieving person. He is the real source of help in this recovery process.

**the gift of our presence and just being there may
be the greatest thing a grieving person needs**

Question:

How can the church or small group better serve someone going through the loss of a loved one? What else besides a dinner for the family or sending a card could be done?

The church can appoint a committee or a small group can consider starting a ministry to those who have recently lost a spouse. Offering a support group to the community can draw those in who have lost a loved one and provide a wonderful ministry for those who have walked through this experience. Often hearing how others have worked through the grieving process can be a help. Being able to share thoughts can help a person to talk through their experience.

Conclusion:

Jesus wept at the tomb of his friend Lazarus. Theologians may debate over the reasons Jesus wept, but we do get a glimpse into the heart of God in this story. God does identify with those who have lost someone close. He watched his own Son die.

For the believer, the truth of God's word can bring real comfort. Psalm 34:18 states that God will be near to those who have a broken heart. No one has to walk "through the valley of the shadow of death" alone. To have a shadow there must be some type of light to cast the shadow. How wonderful to know that when a person walks through the valley of the shadow of the death with a loved one, that they are not alone. Jesus, the light of the world, is near to them, casting a light for them to see so that they can keep walking and living. The survivor's life does not end and God still has a reason for them to live. For a believer, there is no death but only a change of residency. The death of a loved one is not the end of life; it is only a part of life that can introduce us to a closer relationship with the Lord! For those who have lost a child to death, note the words of David, who also lost a child. In II Samuel 12:23, David said, "I shall go to him, but he shall not return to me." We will see our loved ones again in eternity. The last enemy that will be destroyed is death (I Corinthians 15:54-55)!

You cannot only *survive* the death of a spouse but, with God's help, you can *thrive* in life with a greater message of grace and beauty that only the Lord can give. You can *Finish Life Strong* because the Lord is the strength of your life (Psalm 27:1).

Personal Application:

What will you do to prepare yourself for this experience and how can you help others going through the loss of a spouse?

Practical matters: Will completed. Power of attorney, Health directive, Financial interests

_____

_____

Spiritual matters: Unforgiveness issues, Restoration issues Prayer needs

_____

_____

Hot Topic Coming Up:

As a follow up to this study, an issue of interest to many second-halfers is "What about remarrying after the death of a spouse? Is it a blessing or should 'Danger—beware'" signs be posted? Let's find out....

Chapter Six

Can There Be Love After the Death of a Mate?

A True Story:

Reverend Bill Baker and Beverly had been married for 47 years. They had been involved in ministry for many years. They raised a family, pastored churches, and he served his church denomination as a leader.[19] They had enjoyed serving the Lord together. However, as they planned and progressed toward retirement, Beverly became ill and, after a lengthy illness, went home to be with the Lord.

Bill was approaching his retirement years and now he was suddenly alone. He found himself working late and coming home as late as possible to avoid their large and empty house. His district position with his denomination kept him busy during the week and he often traveled on weekends to speak at churches.

Several years went by and Bill's 50th high school graduation reunion was approaching. Bill and Beverly had looked forward to going to this special reunion and he had anticipated the gathering as an opportunity to share his faith. Now, with the prospect of going alone, he thought he would feel out of place.

Bill and Beverly often enjoyed attending their class reunions together with another couple, Kenneth and Barbara Lemmon. Barbara's husband had died suddenly...they had been married for 48 years.

When the phone rang and Bill Baker asked if Barbara would consider going to the reunion with him, not as a couple but in honor of their mates, she said she thought that would be a good tribute and they would not feel out of place going alone. The event came and they went together but really did not spend that much time with each other as they mingled with the other classmates and each shared their recent loss with old friends. The evening ended and both felt relieved the event was over.

The following Monday, Bill was surprised to receive a beautiful fruit basket at the office with a note from Barbara thanking him for a wonderful time at the reunion. Bill's interest grew as he thought of this friend of many years. They soon began seeing each other on a regular basis, and in just a few months started a new marriage and a new life together.

The question is often asked "Can a person find real love after the death of their mate?" Bill and Barbara Baker answer the question with a resounding *yes*. A person *can* love again; they are proof!

An interesting side note: Bill and Barbara Baker had known each other for many years. They both had enjoyed wonderful marriages and families with other spouses. However, Barbara was the **first** person Bill had dated when they were in high school together. And who was the **first** person Barbara ever allowed to kiss her? Well, you guessed it; it was Bill. Over 50 years had passed but they are together again.

The idea of remarriage brings up a lot of questions for second-halfers who find themselves alone after having spent most of their life married. Do I want to get married again? Where would I start looking for a mate? Who would want to marry someone as old as I am? What would my children think if I started dating? Could I trust another person? How did they treat their former spouse? Are they after my money? Do they have money?

Discussion:

Discuss some of these questions, or others that a person would need to consider if they were to have an opportunity to get married again.

_____

_____

Word Faith:

Genesis 2:18 Proverbs 18:22

Question:

How old were you when you were married the first time? Did you have any premarital counseling? Would premarital counseling have helped you to have been better prepared for marriage? How did you start your married life (house, car, furniture, etc)?

_____

_____

Why do you think that parents usually arranged marriages in Biblical times (as they still do in some middle Eastern countries)? Genesis 24 and the book of Ruth give a glimpse into marriage customs in Bible times.

_____

Why do you think marriages lasted longer a generation ago than in today's society?

_____

Where Do I Find Someone?

Question:

Where did you meet your previous spouse?

_____

_____

A True Story:

Bill and Mary, Jim and Sally, Leroy and Opal, (not their real names) Robert and Grace were all recently married. Three couples were in their 70s and one in their early 80s. All four had something in common besides their recent marriages—all four couples found their new spouses on the Internet! Your great-grandparents could not imagine finding a wife through a computer! To them it might sound like using the old mail–order–bride service.

all four couples found their new spouses on the internet!

Today, there are many services that offer opportunities to meet single second-halfers. Online services like eHarmony and some christian dating services offer a way for people to meet. Some churches have singles group meetings. Certainly church can be a great place to meet those who are seeking companionship.

What Should You Look for in a Prospective Spouse?

Make a list of some qualities you think a person considering getting married in the second half of life should look for in another person.

Some things a person may want to consider: Look at the person's previous marriage relationship. Were they happy? How did they treat each other? Talking with the person's family members, or people who know the other person, can give insight into their personality. Of course, no one truly knows someone until they live with them but lifelong friends who will give an honest evaluation can help a person to be better informed and, thus, have a better chance to make the right decision. The old saying "Love is blind" can be followed up with "but marriage is an eye opener!" Most second-halfers should move slowly and cautiously when considering a new relationship.

Humor:

An older man told his buddy that he was considering marrying a friend he had met recently.
"Is she good looking?" asked his friend.
"No," the man replied.
"Is she rich?" his friend continued?
"No," was the reply.
"Well, is she really smart?" his friend pressed for an answer.
"No," the man answered.

"Well, why are you marrying her then?" his friend asked.

The prospective groom smiled and replied, "Well, she can still drive!"

Practical Issues to Consider in a New Marriage:

Here is a list of things that a couple considering marriage may want to discuss **before** the marriage:

Finances:

Should we have a prenuptial agreement? Should we keep separate checking accounts? What about a will?

Usually a couple considering marriage should have a strong enough commitment to each other that the "two should become one" vow includes all areas of life. Often prenuptial agreements set the stage for marriage problems. However, most financial counselors agree that if there is a large sum of money and other investments involved, there are times that a prenuptial agreement can be the best course for a second-half couple. Money disagreements are one of the major causes of divorce and a wise couple should be in agreement about how money will be handled before they say, "I do." Both the man and woman should be involved in the finances of a marriage. The couple should be able to discuss finances freely and be in agreement on major financial decisions.

Question:

Do you know of any couples where only one person controlled all of the finances in the family? Did that create any problems?

Sex:

Intimacy expectations and limitations should be discussed. With the decay of morals in the U.S., many second-halfers are becoming more open to having sex outside of marriage. For believers who want to please Christ, this is not an option.

Living Arrangements:

Where should a new couple live? If both own houses should one or both be sold? Leaving a familiar home with many memories can be traumatic but with prayer and patience new memories can be created and the saying "Home is where the heart is" can become a reality.

Children:

Adult children can be a source of blessing or conflict in a new marriage. Sometimes children may see the new mate as an intruder and be suspicious of their motives. However, a new couple should set boundaries of involvement for their children to respect. You are starting a new relationship and with God's help you should focus on developing a wonderful marriage. You are starting a new family and becoming one is as true for an older couple as it is for younger couples. Adult children can be encouraged to help create a wonderful atmosphere of love and acceptance and welcome a new mother or father into their lives.

A True Story:

Charles and Mary Stillwell live in Benton, Arkansas. They had been married to other spouses for 43 and 44 years respectively. Mary had been widowed for 4 years and Charles had just lost his wife a few months earlier when a former pastor invited Charles to his wife's 50th birthday party. Charles and Mary met and, after a year of dating and praying for God's will, decided to join their hands and homes in marriage. They each had two sons and two daughters and one of their concerns was how the children would accept a new mother or father. There was some initial resistance from the children but they decided that their lives had a future together and so they were married. In time their children have accepted the new relationship. And Charles and Mary, at 76 and 74 years of age, are involved in missions and their local church. One daughter who was initially opposed to her mother marrying a new "dad" has commented to her mother, "Many women don't have a good husband, Mom, but you have had two!" God can unite not only two people but also two families.

Spiritual Compatibility:

The Bible teaches that believers should not marry unbelievers (II Corinthians 6:14). The unequal yoke could also apply to two Christians who have very different backgrounds, lifestyles, and interests. While both may love the Lord, the many differences can be a source of conflict in a new marriage.

Is there spiritual compatibility and harmony regarding beliefs and values? Church attendance and worship styles should be discussed.

God's love is able to help each person get beyond the differences because "love covers a multitude of sins." However, a wise person should consider and certainly pray about entering a relationship where there are conflicting ideas on spiritual matters. If one person loves the Lord and is totally dedicated to faithfully serving Him and the other person is a casual or uncommitted Christian, that should be a warning sign to proceed very cautiously in a relationship. "Opposites may attract, but then attack" when the opposite ideas become glaring.

Some second-half couples may prefer having a dating relationship for mutual support and fellowship, and decide not to marry for one reason or another. The church should find ways to support these couples and strengthen them as individuals.

Most things that God is involved in require *faith* and no one can be totally prepared for the unexpected changes that emerge in a new relationship. There will be a lot of unanswered questions when contemplating a new marriage. Emotional baggage from a previous marriage should be worked through so that a person feels free to enter a new relationship. This may mean talking with someone to discuss previous issues. Prayer is a *vital* component and should not be neglected because of the excitement of a new relationship. God's blessing on our life is more important than our desire for companionship. He will be a husband to the widow. Involvement in a local church family can provide strength and fellowship for those who are unmarried while traveling the second half of life.

Question:

What are some things the church could do to help second-halfers who begin a new marriage?

_____

_____

How Long Should a Person Wait After the Death of a Spouse Before Considering Dating?

While there is no set time common to all, sufficient time to adjust to being single should be given. Some people think they could not live without a mate. However, before a person can live successfully with another person, they first need to be happy living alone. God knows your needs and if you will seek His will for your life and concentrate on *becoming* the right type of person—rather than *finding* the right person—God may send a new person into your life.

Conclusion:

In the second half of life, God's guidance is needed as much as in the first half ... maybe more. After all, you are getting closer to the finish line and that is where the spiritual race will be won or lost. If God does send a new love into your life, it will require a step of faith for both people. With your hand in God's hand, there may be room for another hand that He gives you.

Chapter Seven

Dealing With Change in the Second Half of Life

Word Faith:

II Corinthians 3:18; I Corinthians 15:51; Hebrews 13:8; Malachi 3:6

The longest topic in this study will discuss some of the many changes and challenges that second-halfers face and how they can approach the future with confidence in an ever changing world.

The chorus to an old gospel song says, "Changed in the twinkling of an _____." (Can you fill in the blank?)

Question:

Can you think of any more songs that talk about change either in this life or the next?

_____

Question:

Have you ever gone back to visit a childhood place only to find it is totally gone or changed so much it is hard to recognize? What we thought was a steep hill as a child turned out to be only a small incline when we are adults! How did seeing all the changes make you feel?

Discuss some good changes and some that you feel could have been better had they stayed the same.

Have you ever heard someone say: "You haven't aged a bit; you don't look any older than when you were in school." While that sounds nice, one can likely assume the other person's eyesight is failing, they are trying to be kind, or they didn't pay much attention to you back in your school days!

Physical Change:

Someone once said, referring to all of the physical changes that take place with age, "Nothing works the way it used to; it either sags, leaks, or falls out!"

As the body ages it goes through a lot of changes. Someone has said that men go through the five B's of changing: *baldness, blindness, bridges, bulges* and *bunions*! Society's anti-aging obsession has created a whole host of businesses, services, and products that are geared to help us maintain, regain, or change our appearance. Not only do our bodies change but society, customs, and lifestyles don't remain the same. What was once taboo in society is often promoted by today's media. Topics that used to make people blush are now advertised freely on television—for all to endure. Yes, the slogan "You've come a long way, baby" is true in an ever-changing America. I'm not sure I like all the changes, how about you?

It may be easier to think of the few things that have not changed during your lifetime—rather than to try to count the many changes you have been through. Can you think of anything on earth that has not changed? I can't! Thank God, He alone remains the same, and we can depend on His faithfulness! Hebrews 13:8

Point to Ponder:

Is God young or is he old? *Neither one!* The Scriptures do refer to Him as the Ancient of Days (Daniel 7:9,13,22). But that is a human term, used to describe God in an understandable way, as being forever the source of wisdom. Since God has no beginning or end, He does not age like the rest of us. He is simply the *I Am*; He never changes! If God is neither young or old, then *everyone* can relate to Him—and God can relate to every person, regardless of age.

Whether changes are welcomed (like many modern conveniences) or come unwillingly (like adding inches around our middle, or other places), second-halfers can lead the way in helping to show that God is always the same and can be depended on through *all* of life. That may be one reason you are still around and reading this book. The Lord wants you to share with others about His mercy and faithfulness to you throughout your lifetime.

Psalm 78:1-6

Praise God that His love remains the same through the passing of years! Your trust in Him through all of life's changes is something worth passing on! Think of the song *Great Is Thy Faithfulness.*

Question:

How can second-halfers make a deliberate attempt to pass on some of their heritage and experiences to the next generations?

Ideas: Speak to the youth leader about sharing with the youth of your church your experience with God and how He has provided for you. You may want to do this with another person. Ask some of the youth group to come to one of your adult meetings. Do something special for them when they come. If you have any second-halfers who served in the military, have an "Honor Night" where veterans bring or wear their uniforms (if they can still fit into them). Invite the young people to come for this. They will be impressed.

In the 1960s, Bob Dylan sang about *The Times They Are a Changing.* See if you can relate to this poem:

Grandma's Rocker

In the dim and distant past
When life's tempo wasn't so fast
Grandma used to rock and sit
Crochet, tat and baby sit

> We could always count on Gram
> Whenever we got in a jam,
>
> But now we can't find her
> She's gone to the gym,
> Exercising to keep slim
> She's surfing the Internet
> Checking her emails,
> Placing a bet or polishing her nails,
>
> Nothing seems to block or stop her
> Now that Grandma's off her rocker!

No doubt about it, times and people have changed. Today, the average age that people become grandparents is 47. [20] Today's young grandparents are more likely to be seen riding a Harley-Davidson, climbing a mountain, or skydiving than sitting in a rocking chair. Second-halfers are on the move!

Discussion Point:

It is possible that some that are studying this guide may have used a telephone that hung on the wall and had a hand crank to ring an operator to make a call. Others may have ridden to town in a wagon drawn by horses, or a Model T or Model A Ford. From an old party line to cell phones, from wagons to fast cars, times have changed.

Why not talk about some of the changes you have seen during your lifetime? Start with communication, travel, food, and clothes. Do you remember when you got your first: telephone, washing machine, television (black and white or color), indoor plumbing? Do you own a computer?

Baby Boomers:

Maybe you are a Baby Boomer and do not relate to most of the things your parents experienced. However, even Baby Boomers have seen a lot of changes. You may not relate to Frank Sinatra but you can relate to the Rolling Stones. But who are the Black Eyed Peas?

Music:

Can you remember seeing the Beatles first appearance on the Ed Sullivan show? What seemed like a wild, mop-topped group of musicians singing *I Want To Hold Your Hand*, now seems tame compared to the heavy metal sound and vulgar lyrics that influence today's generation.

What were some of your favorite songs or artists when you were growing up?

Secular: _____

Church: _____

Technology:

Many Baby Boomers remember black and white television, transistor radios, and the threat of nuclear attack. Advances in technology have forced everyone to try and keep up with changes in communication. The computer and the Internet can take us around the world with the click of a mouse. Baby Boomers who once led the world in change are now being overshadowed by the Baby Busters, Generation Xers, and the Millennials (Gen Y).

The desire to keep one's youthful appearance has spawned a whole fitness and health industry. Many Baby Boomers refuse to accept the reality that they are entering the second half of life. Baby Boomers need to embrace reality and accept this new phase of life as an opportunity to see what God has for them. New challenges and new causes need this generation's involvement. The Lord has been waiting for the Baby Boomers to come of age and get with *His* program! Like Mick Jagger, the Boomer generation may not have been able to find "*Satisfaction*" but at this point in your life you don't have to be "*The Little Old Lady from Pasadena!*" There is something for YOU to do at your age!

It seems like change is something *everyone* has to deal with. While young people seem to like change, many second-halfers can feel that there are too many, too fast. The resulting *information overload* can cause those who are technology challenged to respond, "Enough is enough!" No computers, no cell phones, no ipads or iphones, just talk to me! Opposition to change can appear in many forms.

Not only has society changed, but the church is changing. Some changes are very welcome, like padded pews and air conditioning. Better sound and equipment to help spread the gospel around the world are effectively being used. We can thank God that we have seen dramatic changes in our ability to share the gospel. However, some changes are a challenge. When familiar surroundings, music, and even preaching styles change dramatically, second-halfers can find themselves resistant to them.

Let's listen in to this pastor as he shares some thoughts about change and older adults: "Those old folks can't deal with change. If I move the Communion table, they get upset. If someone sits in *their* seat, they get upset. If we sing fast songs, they're too fast; if we sing slow songs, they're too slow. The music is too loud or it's not loud enough. We can't move the pews out for more comfortable chairs because their great-grandfather built them. How can we make progress?"

Questions:

Are the pastor's complaints valid? Do you know anyplace where this or a similar circumstance occurred? What was the outcome? What are some church's *sacred cows* or things that can cause division if they are changed?

_____

_____

How do you deal with change? Do you like it? Some second-halfers embrace change while others resist any attempt to do something different.

In many churches it may appear that all traditional values and customs are being discarded. What once meant so much to so many has been replaced with the unfamiliar, unproven, and (some would say) unscriptural methods and styles.

Tradition:

Long held traditions and established customs have both their values and their snares. Families often connect through meaningful traditions. Jesus kept certain customs and traditions (Luke 4:16). In the church, tradition has value only if it enhances our understanding of the Lord, provides a framework for the Holy Spirit to move in our lives, and builds unity in the body of Christ. Two traditional ceremonies that Jesus left for the church are Communion and Baptism. Jesus was portrayed by the

Pharisees as anti-tradition because He healed a person on the Sabbath. Jesus was considered a liberal by the ultra-traditionalists who valued their tradition over receiving new truth. They missed the Messiah because they had become more comfortable in maintaining their rituals than in receiving God's fresh revelation of Jesus!

Question:

After reading the following sentence, see if you can come up with some examples of when tradition would be helpful and when it may be harmful. "Lord show us the value of tradition, where it serves and where it is perdition."

A Humorous Story:

Twenty-year-old Mary was cooking a ham for her first Thanksgiving meal as a married person. She dutifully cut the large ham in half as her mother and grandmother had taught her. As she was placing the ham in two pans, her new husband asked why she had cut the ham in half. She responded, "Because that is how my mother showed me and how her mother showed her." Her husband, Bill, still wondered about it since he had never seen it done that way. Thanksgiving day came and as Mary's family gathered at her house, Bill asked Mary's mother about the two pans used to cook the ham.

True to tradition, Mary's mother said, "Because that is how my mother showed me how to do it."

Grandmother was also there so Bill asker her why she always cut the ham in half to cook it. She replied, "Because I never had a pan big enough to hold the entire ham!"

Sometimes tradition can be changed for something better. Not many of us drive the same car, wear the same clothes, or use the same washing machine that we did 40 years ago.

Music Changes:

No topic has had more discussion or brought more contention in the church over the past 20 years than music and changes in worship style. In many churches the piano and organ have been replaced with guitars and drums. Songbooks containing many wonderful and faith-building hymns have been exchanged for new choruses and songs of the day. The rhythms and words that were easy to follow a few years ago are now much more complicated. And the volume is often so loud that it may actually cause physical pain to some second-halfers!

Today, there are some very talented musicians and singers who can lead us into the presence of God. In many churches, the worship team is composed of highly trained and dedicated individuals. However, many in the congregation can be found standing, listening, and watching, but not entering into the new style of worship. This is not just because of a lack of desire to enter into worship, but an unfamiliarity with the words, music, and rhythm of the songs. To some people church has become more entertainment than participation in the worship experience. If everyone is watching a few sing, isn't that better defined as a concert than a worship service?

Dave Weston is the director of the Senior Adult Ministries for the Assemblies of God and an accomplished musician. He shares some of his thoughts on dealing with the changes in church music in his article "Who Stole My Music" (*Primeline*, 2008). "I love the hymns and believe they should be incorporated into the worship experience. However, I also have an appreciation for 'new choruses' that usher the worshiper into the presence of the Almighty."

Since the church is made up of believers of all ages, the music and worship experience should be something all can enter into joyfully. Just as you would not expect a youth group to sing all children's songs (the youth would be offended), a youth-oriented style should not be forced on second-halfers. Dr. Robert Spence, president of Evangel University, uses the phrase "Balance and Blending" to describe a solid, meaningful, musical worship experience. If the church is serious about reaching all generations for Jesus, its people need to learn to enjoy the new without discarding the old. The richness of the past when connected to the freshness of the new can provide the basis for a dynamic worship experience where all are involved and blessed.

If the church is serious about reaching all generations for Jesus, its people need to learn to enjoy the new without discarding the old

God did not stop giving songs to people after the 1800s. Some churches continue to only sing their familiar old hymns. The danger in just singing those songs is: the song leader is singing but many people who know the words by heart are not really worshipping God. Familiarity has made what once was a meaningful experience to become just a routine exercise that many endure but don't enjoy.

God is a God of today and He will give songs through people who are experiencing Him today. Charles Wesley (brother of John Wesley) was greatly criticized by the church world because of the "contemporary" songs he wrote for the church. We need inspired new songs, but we also need to be able to hear and understand the words and experience the truth and message in the songs we sing.

Not only has the style of worship music changed, but the volume of the music can be an issue in today's church. Years ago, preachers tended to speak loud and be animated in their preaching. Many second-halfers attended tent meetings (some even went to brush arbors) and camp meetings were a popular form of worship. If the preacher got loud, hollered, and sweat a lot, he was simply considered an anointed messenger.

Question:

Discuss some of the earlier church meetings you attended. What was the format of the music, preaching, altar services, etc.?

_____.

Some ministers were criticized for their style of preaching and accused of trying to *shout* their message into people's lives, Today, many preachers are more conversational in their delivery. However, loud music has replaced the loud sermon in many locales. In some churches you cannot hear the words because of the volume of the music. Rather than *enjoying* music, many second-halfers are *enduring* the process.

Being a musician, I know what it is to "feel the music" when you are performing. Yet, most good musicians have also learned that it is better to play for the audience (or congregation) than just for their own enjoyment. A musician who records his music must learn to exchange quantity of sound for quality to produce a good recording.

A Church of All Headphones (Is this the future?):

What if everyone had their own headphones with a volume control so they could choose how loud the music was?

I have visited several congregations where people of all ages, including mothers with infants, would wait outside the sanctuary until the loud music was over, and then go in to hear the message.

Most sound experts agree that when the decibel level of music goes above 85 it becomes uncomfortable and can be damaging to the ear. Hearing loss can result. Most rock concerts have a level of 110 decibels. And music levels in many contemporary churches is consistently over 90 decibels! If the music is so loud that you cannot hear yourself singing and making melody in your heart to the Lord, you may have become part of a mob that is yielding to the music and not the Holy Spirit. Most Baby Boomers grew up on loud music. Many of the Baby Boomers have hearing losses. I personally like louder music, but I also recognize that it is not all about me.

The lead guitarist of the rock band Who, Pete Townshend, is warning iPod users they may face hearing loss if they pump up the volume on the devices. The band was known for loud performances during which Townshend used to smash his guitars.

Townshend, 60, said his hearing was irreversibly damaged from using studio headphones, and he now takes 36-hour breaks between recording sessions.

"Hearing loss is a terrible thing because it cannot be repaired," Townshend said on his website. "If you use an iPod or anything like it, or your child uses one, you may be okay. But my intuition tells me there is terrible trouble ahead." (http://www.abelard.org/hear/hear.php#townshend)

Question:

How can second-halfers in the church reach out to and connect with the younger people in the church?

Food for Thought:

Gordon McDonald's book *Who Stole My Church* (Thomas Nelson Publishers, 2007) is an excellent source for those who are dealing with the issues of blending the contemporary and traditional church.[21] Both second-halfers and younger generations would benefit from reading and discussing this book. Often the answer to resolving conflict lies in learning to connect, communicate, and build a relationship with people of varied interests.

In McDonald's book, a story is told of older adults who brought snacks to the worship team's practice. It was a wonderful way to start bridging the gap and soon the younger people became interested in doing some music that the older saints enjoyed.

Become a Coach:

Could you or some in your group become coaches to the young people? A way to launch this idea is for the second-halfers to wear a coach's sweatshirt and whistle to a service or function. This lets the young people see that these adults are excited about sharing their story with them.

Should I Leave the Church?

Change can bring severe conflict and division. Some second-halfers who want to avoid conflict have made a choice to go to another church that has similar interests. Sadly, some have changed their denomination or even stopped going to church and prefer to worship at home rather than become critical of the many changes taking place. While I can understand why some would prefer to do this, believers have a responsibility to be in a church and to be a blessing and influence. God can use you to have a positive influence on the next generation. But if you are not there, who will shape the future?

Point to Ponder:

The church needs everyone: no one should leave a church just because of music. However, it happens. Second-halfers should endeavor to stay engaged and be salt and light for future generations! If what we have is the truth, then learning how to pass on our faith to those following us is important. We should diligently pray that God will give us the right approach, method and attitude in seeking to leave a legacy for others to build upon.

Conclusion:

Sam Walton, founder of Wal-Mart, said: "You can't just keep doing what works one time: everything around you is changing. To succeed, stay out in front of change."

Life is full of changes! The Christian life begins with a change of heart. Jesus came to change not only our future but our present. Change for the sake of change is not necessary. Change for the sake of seeing God's kingdom advanced and individuals drawn closer to the Lord is a mandate we all must embrace.

Truth From a Song:

"As we walk with the Lord in the light of His Word, what a glory He sheds on our way." As both good and bad experiences come in life, every person chooses how they will react. Some see change as a threat, while others see an opportunity. When change comes, with God's help, we can still grow closer to Him. We have the assurance that the Holy Spirit will be with us through every change of life. Prayer can be the process where we seek God for his help in understanding change and how we can be a part of today's church to *Finish Life Strong*!

Concluding Prayer:

A 17th-century Nun's Prayer

Lord, Thou knowest better than I know myself that I am growing older and will someday be old.

Keep me from the fatal habit of thinking I must say something on every subject and on every occasion.

Release me from craving to straighten out everybody's affairs.

Make me thoughtful but not moody, helpful but not bossy.

With my vast store of wisdom, it seems a pity not to use it all, but thou knowest, Lord, that I want a few friends at the end.

Keep my mind free from the recital of endless details: give me wings to get to the point.

I dare not ask for improved memory, but for a growing humility and a lessening cocksureness when my memory seems to clash with memories of others. Teach me the glorious lesson that occasionally I may be mistaken.

Keep me reasonably sweet: I do not want to be a saint, some of them are so hard to live with, but a sour old person is one of the crowning works of the devil.

Give me the ability to see good things in unexpected people.

And give me, O Lord, the grace to tell them so ... Amen!

Chapter Eight

Finding Christ in the Second Half of Life-
Can people past 50 be won to Christ?

A True Story:

Bea was 69 years old when she came to Christ. She had lived a rough life, **45** years of which had been spent in prison. Now, she was out of prison and, as a new believer, she was excited about serving Jesus!

Shirley was 73 years old when she came to Christ. Shirley had led an interesting life. She was married when she was 13 years old. By the time she was 20 years of age, she had five children. Shirley did not know God and went through several tragedies. One of her sons was viciously murdered by his mother-in-law.

Yet, God loved Shirley, and at age 73 she found Jesus as her Savior. Now, in the second half of her life, she wants to help young girls who are in trouble.

Information:

Many studies indicate that the younger a person is, the easier it is to reach them for Christ. They conclude that young hearts tend to be more open to spiritual truth than older people.

I would agree that we should try to reach every boy and girl for Jesus and disciple them in the ways of the Lord. A young heart can be more pliable than that of a person who has been hardened to spiritual truth.

A young life given to Christ has the prospect of more years to serve and worship the Lord. However, I would contest the concept that an older person is too difficult to be reached for Christ. I would like to suggest that the reason we have not seen as many people in the second half of life won to the Lord is the church's lack of diligence in its evangelistic outreach to that group.

Think with me, *How much money has been spent in learning how to reach children for the Lord? A lot! How many books on winning children have been written? Many! How many programs in the church are directed toward winning young people to the Lord? Many!* There are hundreds of camps for young people to attend, boys and girls discipleship programs, youth programs, and studies on how to reach the heart of a child. Christian colleges emphasize educating young people. All of these efforts have the goal of reaching and discipling youth at an early age. We thank God for every effort to reach young souls. They have resulted in millions of boys and girls accepting and learning about Jesus.

Point to Ponder:

Power flows where the money goes!
While the above statement is secular in nature, it does contain a nugget of truth that believers and the church should consider.

Seven Wake-up Questions:

1. Why do so few older people come to know Christ?
2. Are older adults unwilling and too set in their ways to change?
3. Has God abandoned His efforts to reach those who are closer to the finish line of life?
4. How much time and resources have been invested in learning how to reach people in the second half of life?
5. How many books have been written on reaching second-halfers for Christ?
6. How can we touch the hearts of those who have entered into a time of life when changes and challenges may seem overwhelming?
7. What portion of a church budget is devoted to reaching younger people in comparison to reaching second-halfers?

There are millions more people who are adults past 50 years of age than those 18 and under. If the church would spend a portion of its resources and time in learning how second-halfers respond to truth, and then develop programs to address those needs, I believe we would see a large harvest of souls from this group. If there is no work being done in part of the harvest field, can we expect anything to be reaped there? God is faithful. If we plant good seeds in the heart of adult generations, He will honor His Word.

Word Faith:

Acts 2:21; Romans 10:13; John 4:35; Proverbs 29:18

How would you apply these verses to reaching people in the second half of life?

With population trends shifting toward those in the second half, a huge harvest field awaits the church. To be relevant in the 21st century, the church must consider and develop strategies to reach this field. Every segment of the population is difficult to reach for Jesus, but God will give us wisdom and insight if we will pray, prepare, and plan to get involved in the harvest. After all, it is *His* harvest!

> **To be relevant in the 21st century, the church must consider and develop strategies to reach this field.**

A True Story:

Jake was 91 when he found the Lord. His son was helping a pastor work around the church and there were numerous holes in the ground that gophers had dug. "I wish we could get rid of these gophers," lamented the pastor.

"My dad knows how!"

"Really? Have him come down," replied the pastor.

So, 91-year-old Jake came down to the church, applied his secret formula, and dispersed the gophers. A couple of weeks later, as the son was getting ready for church, he noticed that Jake was getting dressed up. "Dad, what are you doing?" asked the man who had not seen his dad go to church for many years.

"I think I better go check on those gophers," Jake replied. The Holy Spirit was drawing Jake and that morning Jake went to church, walked down the aisle, and gave his heart to the Lord. Several years later I checked on Jake and the pastor said he was then 95 years old, took up the offering every week, and helped serve Communion. Yes, people in the second half of life can come to know the Lord and find a place of service.

Question:

Do you know anyone who accepted the Lord in the second half of their life? What issues do you think someone would face who gets saved later in life?

_____

Word Faith:

Joel 2:25
How could this verse apply to a person that comes to faith later in life? _____

Question:

Who do you know who is in the second half of life that you would like to see accept the Lord?

_____

_____

Information:

Let's look at a few ways that God is using to touch lives and bring adults to faith.

Most people in the second half of life come to Christ through first knowing someone else who is a believer. Second-halfers are not necessarily looking for the same kind of thrills and adventures that young people enjoy. Most aren't into going to Six Flags or Disney World and getting turned upside down on a roller coaster. A few second-halfers still enjoy that thrill, but, most prefer personal relationships and talking about what is going on in their life and families. Second-halfers like to learn new things and use the skills they have gained over a lifetime. Baby Boomers grew up in a generation that was cause oriented and many are still interested in making a difference in their world.

Point to Ponder:

Second-halfers can be won to the Lord by establishing meaningful relationships with them, recognizing their abilities, and engaging them in projects that can help bring positive change.

Point of Action:

Think of those you listed as needing Christ. What can you do to see them come to faith? Pray for them, yes. But after prayer, then what? How can you develop a better relationship with them? Do you know their birthday, the names of their children or grandchildren? Perhaps once a month (you may need to write it down on a calendar) you could take part of a day and make it an evangelistic outreach to make a contact with that person. Spending time over a cup of coffee or meal is a great way to show them the love of God. Isn't that how God showed his love toward us—by sending Jesus to spend time with us?

Some churches have specific outreach programs that target people in the second half of life. Educational programs such as Learning the Computer after 50 or How to operate your cell phone, and others can help the second-halfer learn to navigate life in an ever changing technological society. Classes on health, financial planning, grand parenting, taking care of elderly family members and other relevant topics can attract people who would not otherwise come to church.

Churches can offer to help families who live miles away from loved ones by contacting their family member. When a church becomes known in a community as having programs and ministry to older second-halfers, just sit back and see what God does!

Developing programs that consider the needs of the community as well as second-halfers can be extremely beneficial. It can result in new ministries for people in the church and help to reach one of the largest mission fields in America outside the church.

Baby Boomers:

The sheer magnitude of the numbers of people born between 1946 and 1964—76 million—deserves special prayer and planning. This group has always been a demanding and decisive trend-setting segment of the population. Many who protested America's involvement in Vietnam, demanded equal rights, and threw aside traditional moral values, are now coming into their second half. They were the first generation to be raised on rock-and-roll music. In order for the church to reach this group, it must be aware of their interests and needs. Baby Boomers can't be won with the same methods that reach older second-halfers. The gospel is relevant to every age, but knowing how to apply the message to a group takes prayer and planning. The priority must be to reach souls for Jesus, not convert people to our personal interests. The chart at the end of this chapter lists some of the differences between the Baby Boomer and the Builder generations. Reaching both groups for the Lord requires the church to understand the different mindsets and develop ministries to present the gospel in ways that each can understand.

Baby Boomers in their pre-retirement or retirement years bring with them many professional skills that a local church would do well to enlist in God's work. Leadership skills can be used to help the church develop new strategies and programs in reaching out to the community. All efforts must be saturated with prayer to make sure that the church's direction is where the Lord wants it to go. Education alone will not accomplish God's will or win the world. However, God anointed and directed education can certainly help to move the church forward and reach people for Jesus!

Most in the Baby Boomer generation are still active—in work, raising grandchildren, relationship issues, or taking care of elderly parents. A church can assist and reach out to those in this group by offering classes and assistance with their challenges. Asking the Baby Boomers to help you in short-term special projects can be effective. Whether they are reaching out to children or other second-halfers, this may create an interest which becomes a passion to change the world.

Question:

What could your church do to reach out to the Baby Boomers in your area? What issues are they facing that you could address with ministry?

———————————————————————————————————

———————————————————————————————————

Baby Boomers like cars, music, sports, and money—and they want to be healthy. Consider hosting a classic car show, a music event, financial seminar, or other information-based workshops. These can provide tools to help Baby Boomers and result in greater interest in the Lord's agenda! Since most of them are still very active, getting them to commit to a long-term area of service (such as teaching a class, or being over a group of boys) may not be feasible. However, they may be willing to do an occasional special event or be involved in a project that has an end in sight. Utilize the Baby Boomers' skills and assets, and keep praying that God will send in additional workers.[22]

A True Story:

Jack Fisher lives in Bakersfield and is a Baby Boomer. He had been raised in church but never took the things of God seriously. He shares: "I was raised in the church in my youth but there was always that something in the back of the mind, an awareness of a need unfulfilled, an unknown about life or finding its purpose. By 1967, as I went off to college, I had pretty much given up on church and God. I was having a grand time banging on the drums and running wild with the college crowd." While Jack and his wife, Venus, were living in Thailand they met missionaries who witnessed to them and loved them to Jesus. At age 53 he surrendered to Christ. Now he is active in his local church and studying a Bible correspondence program. God saves Baby Boomers!

A lady in Missouri who was about 55 years old told me she was going to live to be at least 100. I asked her why, and she responded, "I lived my first 50 years for the devil and now I want to live at least that many years serving the Lord!" I hope she makes it!

People of all ages are getting saved in the second half of life—and finding new joy and purpose.

Word Faith:

II Peter 3:9
God is still unwilling that any should perish. Is the church? Is the church willing to learn what it takes and make the necessary sacrifices to see that *all* the harvest is reached?

Conclusion:

Why not pray for the church to get a new vision of how to reach second-halfers for Christ? Could you be part of the answer to that prayer? Pray by name for those who you would like to see come to Christ.

Additional Insight:

Is there a difference within members of the second-half generations? Yes! There are two main second-half groups—the Builders and the Baby Boomers.

How does each group view the world, the church, and themselves? Note the fundamental differences.

There are exceptions to the following list, but these are general characteristics of each group.

The Builders

1   Born before 1946
2   Respond well to teaching
3   Sacrifice of self
4   Focus on group and community goals
5   Common values and ethics
6   Used words like "we, us, pull together"
7   Loyal to the institution (job, school, marriage)
8   Followed rules, respected authority
9   Resistance to change
10 Common religious heritage
11 "When We All Get to Heaven"
12 Financial view: save, save, save
13 Spiritual view: "What can I do for God?"
14 Church view: "How can I help the church?"

The Boomers

1   Born 1946-1964
2   Respond well to interaction
3   Self realization
4   Focus on individual goals
5   Individual values and ethics
6   Words like "me, mine, I"
7   Loyal to individual goals

8   Question authority
9   Insistence on change
10 Minimal religious heritage
11 Looking out for number one
12 Financial view: spend, spend, spend
13 Spiritual view: "What can God do for me?"
14 Church view: "What can the church do for me?"

While the Builder generation helped to build a great America, they still need God. They do respond to sincere compassion and they enjoy friendships that show respect for their contributions. Most want to belong to something bigger than they are.

While the Baby Boomer generation sought to change America, they still need God. Their desire to make a positive change in the world can be a way to connect them to a church that is involved in community, world evangelization, and social issues. Addressing the personal as well as the spiritual needs of the Baby Boomer can help to show them the church is relevant to their life.

Chapter Nine

Growing Spiritually in the Second Half of Life

The final study topic in this series is how to keep your spiritual life alive and growing so you enjoy God's presence and He can use you in the second half of life. One of the signs that someone is dying is that they have stopped learning. Someone has said, "When our memories exceed our dreams, we begin to die." God still has a dream for the last half of life and once you see it, life can have new meaning. This last topic will help you keep running life's spiritual race to the finish line—where the race is won or lost. If Satan could not stop you from serving the Lord when you were young, then he may be saving his biggest tests for you in the second half of life. Thankfully, God also promises as much grace and strength as is needed to *Finish Life Strong!* I hope this study will stir all of our hearts to keep striving to win the prize of the high calling of God in Jesus Christ. We have also included an interesting project that will help each reader apply God's Word to some of your major life experiences. You have a story to tell!

Word Faith:

Psalm 92:12-14
God wants every believer to continue to bear spiritual fruit throughout all of life. This scripture holds God's promise that those who stay close to Him will continue to have a productive life! While

some things will change in the second half of life, I believe it should be one of your most spiritually rewarding times.

Point to Ponder:

In the lifetime of a fruit tree, when does the fruit appear? When it is first planted, in springtime, or after its growth and maturity? The normal growing process goes something like this: First, the seed is planted, then a shoot breaks forth from the ground. In time a tree rises and then limbs appear. Soon leaves begin to sprout and finally, at the end of a long process, the fruit is formed, grows, and ripens. Could God be saying to second-halfers that he looks for fruit at the end of our life? Are we bearing fruit in our older age?

Fruit is only good if it is shared with others. The tree does not consume its own fruit; it is for others to enjoy. God has brought you to this point in your life so that others may taste of God's goodness in your life. That truth should influence all second-halfers to keep seeking, serving, and sharing God's love!

Illustration:

Some in their second half can get the attitude that, since they are older and more mature, they do not have to go to church as much as others. Occasional church attendance sets a bad example and can be dangerous to our spiritual health!

A pastor visited a man who had not been attending church for sometime. It was winter and as the pastor entered the man's house he felt the warmth of a fire in the fireplace. As they sat talking the man remarked to the pastor, "I suppose you've noticed I have not been attending church as much as I should?" The pastor silently reached with the tongs to the fire and took out a red hot ember and placed it on the hearth. Both men sat gazing at the glowing ember as it changed from red hot to orange, then yellow then became black. As the temperature cooled, the ember gave off a final gasp of smoke and then just lay there. The man spoke first. "I get your message, pastor. I'll be in church this Sunday!"

Unless physical limitations or other circumstances prevent it, *every* believer should go and support the church with their presence!

Question:

What was the pastor's silent message to the man? How does it relate to spiritual growth and fervency for the Lord?

_____

_____

The B-I-B-L-E ... is it still the book for me? Remember that song?

It is important that the Word of God continue to hold an attraction to second-halfers. For those who have served the Lord for a number of years there can be the temptation to seldom read and study the Word of God because they have heard it so much.

There are daily temptations and challenges that everyone faces. Like oxygen, your spiritual man needs God breath every day. "God breathed into man the breath of life, and he became a living soul" (Genesis 2:7). This spiritual air can come in a variety of ways.

Question:

What are some different ways you can feed your spirit every day?

_____

_____

Word Faith:

I Peter 2:2; Romans 10.17, Matthew 5.1, II Peter 3.18, II Timothy 4:6-8

Suggestions for studying the Bible and prayer:

1. Read a chapter in Proverbs each day and you will complete the Book of Wisdom in one month. Billy Graham has practiced this for years.
2. Study what the Bible says about a topic of special interest. Examples: trust, faith, fear, temptation, money, prayer, tongue, anger.
3. Study the life of an interesting Bible person: Peter, Paul, Esther, Noah, Job.
4. Keep a prayer list that you pray over every day. You may have several lists—one for family needs, one for friends and

your church, one for those with physical needs, and one for missionaries and needs around the world. Pray each day over a different list.

5. Start a prayer chain of people in your church who are available to pray when an emergency develops. God answers prayer but we must actually do the praying before He steps in!

6. Keep a card with special needs on the visor of your car. While driving and stopped at a red light (which can last for two to three minutes), look up and pray over those needs while waiting for the light to change. Don't get so lost in praying you forget to go on green! "Watch and pray" should be your guideline!

7. When you pass or hear an emergency vehicle, pray for the person and family involved. Pray for the person in the car next to you. You never know what needs they have, and your prayer could make a difference!

Plans to continue studying what the Bible says about life at every age is important. Prayer is a wonderful opportunity for second-halfers to develop a powerful tool that God will use. Your family needs your prayers! Your pastor and church need your prayers! You will be surprised how God answers your prayers and your relationship with Him develops.

Perhaps you and a friend could pray together or at least check on one another throughout the week as to how you each are doing in your devotion time. Being accountable to another person can help one to keep pursuing God.

Involvement in a local church is important. Purposing to stay connected and involved is an important component in spiritual growth. The church needs *you*. Ask God how He wants you to be involved in the life of your church and community.

Learning From Life's Experiences:

Second-halfers have something younger people don't have. Experiences! Looking back on 50, 60, 70, or more years brings floods of memories to mind. Hearing just a phrase of an old song can instantly transport you back to a younger time in life. A long life yields a lot of experiences. Many of them were great and their memory is treasured. But, to be honest, no one gets out of life without having some rough times! God seems to make sure that every life has its difficulties. Whether it is to help us focus on the eternal, learn something to help someone else, or see the power of God at work in our lives, trials and tests are a part of every life. Having experiences without learning from them can just be frustrating.

A True Story:

A story is told of Robert Schuller (of Crystal Cathedral fame). He was asked to speak at a gathering of farmers in a Midwestern state. Born in Iowa, Schuller had been gone many years and had already built the beautiful glass cathedral in Garden Grove, California. (I have sat in their sanctuary and, through the glass, watched traffic on the freeway going by on a Sunday morning.) As Schuller contemplated what he would say to these hardened farmers who had been going through severe drought, and who were concerned about losing their farms, he thought it somewhat strange that he, living in busy southern California, would be asked to speak to a group of farm families. What would they have in common? When Schuller rose to speak that morning he looked out over the crowd at the weather-beaten faces of people who for years had toiled in the soil to help feed a nation and world. These were simple, honest, hardworking people who were going through some hard circumstances. Some in the crowd may have wondered what this suburban preacher would have to say to them in their time of need.

Schuller began his speech by saying, "Tough times don't last, but tough people do!" With those simple words, Schuller connected with the crowd and, as he shared some of his own struggles, success joined hands with sorrow, prosperity met poverty, and hope was instilled in people's hearts.

Question:

How would you apply Schuller's message—"Tough times don't last, but tough people do!"—to life in the second half?

_____

_____

Word Faith:

Luke 9:62; Matthew 10:22; Galatians 6:9; Revelation 2:10

Point to Ponder:

The story of Joseph (Genesis 37 and 39-50) provides insight into learning from life's experiences. Joseph had some great moments of success and prosperity, rising to be second in command in all the nation of Egypt. Yet, he also had gone through some tough and trying times earlier in life. Being mocked by his family and sold into slavery would not be on anyone's wish list, but somehow Joseph managed to keep his eyes on God and his heart in tune with his maker.

Question:

Why do you think tough times cause us to focus on the Lord more than when we are experiencing good times?

Joseph also spent time in prison where again things were difficult. Later, looking back over his life, he would tell his brothers that, although they had meant to do him harm and evil when they sold him into slavery, God had a bigger and better plan for him (Genesis 50: 20). God had brought good out of a bad situation and ultimately used Joseph to save the nation of Israel.

Dynamic Revelation:

Your Story is Important

Over your lifetime God has had a big picture for you. Jeremiah 29:11 speaks of His thoughts and plans for you. Satan also wants to turn your eyes from looking to God to looking at yourself and living with a small (me only) view of life.

One of the best ways to grow spiritually is to develop a *life message* and testimony. The project below can help a person gain insight and perhaps help to answer some long held questions—by reviewing a lifetime that may appear to have been filled with many reverses. This project can help apply a lesson that God would have us to learn through life's negative experiences. I doubt that when Joseph was going through some of his tough times he initially saw the hand of God in his circumstance. He was just trying to survive—being thrown into a pit, taken captive by the Midianites, being tempted by Potiphar's wife, or spending time in jail. Likewise, when we go through a trial, we may not always feel like singing, "Something good is going to happen today!" However, like Joseph in his second half, we can look back and say with him, "This thing could have brought evil and ruin into my life, but I am going to see what God was doing in that circumstance and the good that will come of it" (Genesis 50:20). Perhaps God protected you or spared you from further harm, even death, at one time in your life. Somehow, even if you did not realize it at the time, you got through the situation! Now, let's see how God was with you or how He helped you at the time.

In this project you will try to discern what the lesson from life's experiences could be. This project can help you to develop a *life message* and testimony that may encourage others in your family or church. At the very least, it will help you to apply God's Word to your life story and may give you answers for some long unanswered questions you have had. A portion of the song *Through it All* by Andrae Crouch says it perfectly:

> I thank God for the mountains and I thank Him for the
>
> valleys and I thank Him for the storms
>
> He's brought me through!
>
> For if I never had a problem,
>
> I'd never know my God could solve them
>
> And I'd never know what faith in God could do

When you can thank God for the experience you went through (not for the heartache, pain, or sin that may have caused the situation), you can see that God was there, that you were not alone. Now you have a *life message* worth sharing!

Personal Project for Spiritual Growth:

Make a list of some of the most challenging things that have happened to you in your life.

It may take several pages for some. Since we should learn from all of life list both good and bad events. Leave space on the opposite side of the page for comments (see example). You can start with childhood experiences, then school, marriage and family, divorce, death of a loved one, work, etc. Maybe you suffered a broken leg or a broken heart. Write it down. Then find a Bible verse that could apply to that experience. You can work with a friend and make this a team project, although each person should do their own list. You may want to plan to bring your list back to the next meeting, with at least two or three things to discuss.

EXPERIENCE-GOD'S LESSON (Scripture and comment):

1.

2

3.

Growing spiritually in the Lord will not just happen. Weeds happen, but good fruit takes work. It's never too late to start doing what is right! Don't give up!

Word Faith:

Philippians 1:6; Hebrews 10:35,36; Hebrews 12:1,2; Galatians 6:9

A Final True Story to Help Finish Life Strong:

The 1992 Summer Olympics had one of the most memorable events ever witnessed. Derrick Redmond was representing Great Britain in the 440-meter race. He was one of the favorites to win the race and he started quickly. He was in the best shape of his life and hopes were high for his chance at a gold medal. However, as he passed the halfway mark, his leg began to cramp and Derrick pulled up lame with a hamstring muscle injury. In severe pain Derrick fell to the track as the other runners continued the race. All of his dreams came crashing to the ground as he knelt on the ground with his head down. Suddenly something happened. From within his heart came the will to finish the race. He stood up and began hobbling down the track toward the finish line.

At first the thousands in the stands were amazed and then applause began to build to a crescendo. Derrick continued the race. But, the next thing that happened was even more amazing. A man came out of the stands and, brushing past security, he joined the young athlete, putting his arm around him. Together they kept their eyes on finishing the race. The man who risked arrest to join the runner was Derrick Redmond's father, who later said, "We started his career together and I thought it was only fitting that we should end it together." Derrick Redmond's father's love for his son was the motivating factor for joining his son on the track! Nothing was going to keep him from going to his child who needed him at that moment.

You can watch this epic moment on YouTube by typing in "Derrick Redmond."

It always moves me to tears to watch this touching depiction of a father's love.

Application:

All of us are in a race for our lives. We are doing the best we can to finish the race that God has set before us. But life has a way of sometimes knocking us to the ground. Whatever the reason, or the problem, you may feel at times like you have been knocked down in the Christian race. You may even feel like giving up.

How wonderful to know that we are not alone in our race. Our Heavenly Father will come out of the stands of heaven, down to our side, lift us back to our feet and will help us finish the race. Like Derrick Redmond's father, our Heavenly Father also says to us: *We started this race together when you accepted Jesus into your life. And we will finish the race together.* With His help all of us can finish life's race! We may be limping, we may be struggling, but we can *finish!*

Prayer:

Lord, I believe that the second half of life can be more exciting than the first half. I don't want to stop growing in my life of following You. As I continue running the race You have for me, let me not get discouraged by some of the changes that occur to me or my friends. Even when I feel knocked down in the race, and regardless of the circumstances, I know that You have promised to help me. I commit the rest of my years to You to help make them the best of my years. With Your help I will *Finish Life Strong!* Amen.

Chapter Ten

What Others Are Doing-
Stories of Hope and Inspiration

Word Faith:

Psalms 92:12-14

God's Word says that second-halfers can continue to be fruitful throughout all of life. As a matter of fact, this could be the period of life when we bear "much fruit" as Jesus taught in John 15.

Throughout this book we have shared numerous stories of people who have been touched by God or who are touching others for God in their second half. Here are some others we have met across the country who have done something significant in their second half! I hope these will challenge and inspire you to see that you, too, can make a difference.

Owen Carr is in his late 80s. He has enjoyed a wonderful life of ministry in several states and around the world. He has pastored a number of thriving churches and helped to begin a national program that impacted thousands of young people. He helped to start a Christian television station in Chicago that reaches out to millions. His life has been fulfilling and rewarding for him and Priscilla, his wife. However, Owen Carr did not believe that God was through with him and, at 83 years of age, started a new church plant. Now, at 88 years old, and along with his son, David, and their wives, Owen pastors a wonderful group of people at Grace Assembly in Springfield, Missouri.

Eighty-nine-year-old Joseph Prettyman and his wife, Carolyn, pastor Christian Assembly in Seal Beach, California. He tried retirement at 65 but says it wasn't for him. Howard and Charlotte Goss serve as their associates. Pastor Prettyman says that Howard is his youth pastor. Howard is 93 years old! Now that's a youth pastor! The church they pastor also had the oldest living person in California, a lady who was 112 years old!

George O. Wood, now 70 years of age, is leader of the Assemblies of God fellowship that has over 64-million adherents. His dynamic and innovative leadership is helping that movement to reach out around the world with the gospel.

Eddie Glover of Conway, Arkansas, has loved to play baseball all of his life. At 75, he continues to play in tournaments across the country. That is, when he is not working at the Army National Guard at Camp Robinson where he has worked the past 43 years (and currently works part time). Eddie is an excellent Bible teacher who loves God.

Claude Cowan worked at Carter-Waters construction for 21 years. He also served as a volunteer pastor for Senior Adults at a church in Independence, MO. Considering what he wanted to do with the rest of his life he felt God calling him to full time service. At age 60 he and his wife Bonnie, became pastors for the first time and now serve the congregation at Eastpoint Family Church in Kansas City, MO.

Jack Chancellor of Sierra Vista, Arizona, thought his days of pastoring were over. He was content serving as an associate and ministering to the senior adults in a larger church. Then a new opportunity opened for him and today he finds himself, at 81, pastoring and reviving a church in Tombstone, Arizona. You remember hearing about Tombstone? That's where Sheriff Wyatt Earp had a gunfight at the O.K. Corral. Pastor Jack and his group are still fighting the enemy, only now they are in the good fight of faith for the Lord!

Marguerite Tillman was 88 years old when we first met her. They called her the "street preacher." She was small in stature but a dynamic person who had served God for many years. With age came some limitations, but she still had a desire to lead people to Jesus. At 91 years of age, Marguerite was still going down to help in a mission and handing out tracts on the street.

Winner of 10 World Titles in racquetball, Jerry Northside is 75 years young. Jerry still helps people stay in shape by sharing good advice such as this: "Good nutrition, eating less, eating slower, and staying away from the bad things that can negatively impact the body is a key to staying physically fit." Jerry and his doubles partner recently won another World Title at Santa Fe, New Mexico, taking first place in both the 65-69 age range and the 70-75 category. Jerry has also won many state and national titles. He has helped to train many world-class athletes and designed athletic clubs. Jerry also loves God and is active in his local church in Prescott, Arizona. Thanks, Jerry, for showing and encouraging us to *Finish Life Strong* and active. Would you want to play against him?

Maude was 82-years-old and had become homebound due to physical limitations. She had been very active in her church for many years and now she thought, *What can I do?* One morning while in prayer she said, "Lord, I still want to do something for you, please show me what it is." At that moment she felt the Lord tell her to look under the table she was sitting next to. Her telephone book was on it. Maude started calling every person in her small town and asking them two questions—"Do you know Jesus?" and "Is there anything I can pray with you about?"

You can imagine what many of the responses were like. However, occasionally she spoke with someone who had recently lost a spouse or a child, and they were looking for help. Other times she reached someone whose marriage was falling apart and who was desperate for encouragement. It took Maude two years to get through her phone book but at the end of that time she had personally led 200 souls to Jesus. Wow! What an example!

Speaking of using a phonebook, a lady in Illinois goes through her phone book and prays over people's names. She also sends out tracts in the mail to those she feels God impresses on her heart. She has sent out thousands of letters over the years. What is the cost of a soul? A stamp! I believe she will have a reward in heaven.

Hilton Griswold is 90 years young. He traveled as the pianist for the Blackwood brothers quartet from 1940-1950. Is he slowing down today? Not Hilton, he still gives 16 music programs a month, teaches a Sunday school class, travels extensively for meetings, (he drives), and has a television program seen across the country on cable and the internet called "Inspiration Time." When asked how he is doing he simply says, "Still-a-going!" I believe it, don't you? Look him up on You Tube.

For over 50 years 85 year old Glenn Martin of Springfield, MO has mentored hundreds of young boys. Working one on one he has taught many to read and given them valuable skills to live successfully.

Why not add a personal story you know?

If you know of an inspiring adult who God is using, I would love to hear their story.

johnheide2002@yahoo.com
or:
813 Oak St. 10-139
Conway, AR 72032
Phone: 417-838-0059
www.50alive.com

I would like to acknowledge the following people who have inspired and encouraged me in pursuing ministry to those in the Second-Half of life: Judy my loving wife, who has traveled with me sharing this message and to a very special Aunt Shirley.

To a multitude of special friends too numerous to name who have helped us on this journey my deepest love and respect.

To Janice Moore who helped create and design the cover for this book . . . a special thanks!

For more copies of this book or for quantity discounts call:
417-838-0059 or go to: www.inspiringvoices.com

To have John Heide come to speak at your church, conference
or workshop contact the author at:
Johnheide2002@yahoo.com or 813 Oak St. 10-139, Conway, AR 72032

Endnotes

Introduction

[1]   U.S. Department of Health and Human Services, National Institutes of Health. National Institute on Aging Projected Centenarians for the First 50 years of 2000. 2000 72,000 2010 131,000

[2]   *The New York Post*, July 24, 2011; http://www.nypost.com/p/news/local/first_same_sex_weddings_take_place_Cnzs5B8JcW6EC6Esu04oOJ

[3]   *Pentecostal Evangel*, July 21, 2011, p. 27

Chapter One

[4]   Lewis Jackson, pastor, Vivian, Louisiana

[5]   The Finisher, Jan Kinney, Intermedia Publishing Company, 2009, pg. 149.

[6]   Nola Ochs; http://abcnews.go.com/GMA/LifeStages/story?id=3167970

[7]   MAPS division, Assemblies of God U.S. Missions; http://usmaps.ag.org/

Chapter Two

[8]   http://www.ssa.gov/history/lifeexpect.html

[9]   John Wooden, *Washington Post*, June 5, 2010.

[10] *My Utmost for His Hightest*, Oswald Chambers, September 1.

Chapter Three

[11] http://www.gu.org/OURWORK/Grandfamilies/ GrandfamiliesStatistics.aspx

[12] http://genealogy.about.com/od/journaling/tp/legacy_journals. htm

[13] www.50alive.com

Chapter Four

[14] *Springfield News-Leader,* June 1, 2011 Tara Muck

[15] http://www.nimh.nih.gov/health/index.shtml; "Depression"

[16] Illinois Department of Public Health; http://www.idph.state. il.us/about/chronic/Suicide-Older_Adults.pdf

[17] Global Teen Challenge Programs; http://www.globaltc.org/

Chapter Five

[18] http://www.harvestenterprises-sra.com/The%20Holmes-Rahe%20Scale.htm

Chapter Six

[19] Reverend Bill Baker served as the Superintendent of the Southern Missouri District of the Assemblies of God.

Chapter Seven

[20] "When grandparents become grandparents" http://grandparents. about.com/od/grandparentdemographics/a/Demographics.htm

[21] Who Stole My Church, Gordon McDonald, Thomas Nelson Publishers, 2007.

Chapter Eight

[22] For a more in-depth study on reaching and incorporating the Baby Boomer and beyond into the life of the church, I recommend Amy Hanson's book *Baby Boomers and Beyond*, A Leadership/Network publication, 2010.